AWAKEN

TO YOUR

OWN CALL

AWAKEN
TO YOUR
OWN CALL

EXPLORING
A Course in Miracles

JON MUNDY

CROSSROAD · NEW YORK

1994

The Crossroad Publishing Company
370 Lexington Avenue, New York, NY 10017

Copyright © 1994 by Jon Mundy

Printed in the United States of America

Library of Congress Cataloging-in-Publication Data
Mundy, Jon.
    Awaken to your own call : exploring A course in miracles / Jon Mundy.
    p. cm.
    ISBN 0-8245-1387-8 (pbk.)
    1. Course in miracles. 2. Spiritual life. I. Title.
BP605.C68M86 1994
299'.93—dc20
                                93-39494
                                CIP

To My Mother,
Milly Mundy

*You will awaken
to your own call,
for the Call
to awake
is within you.*

—A Course in Miracles
T.194; T-11.VI.9:1

Contents

Part II
Application of the *Course*

Part III
All about Nothing:
The Metaphysics of Miracles

Part IV
Nothing Real Can Be Threatened

Acknowledgments

First and foremost, thanks to Diane Berke, my partner in the founding of Interfaith Fellowship and *On Course* magazine, for her ever-present love and devotion, for her conscientious reading of this work, and for her constructive comments and suggestions.

Thank you to our assistants Ruth Murphy and Meribeth Seaman, who have each spent many hours in editing, and to Christina Serra, who carefully checked the references.

Thank you to Sara Emrie Brown for her friendship and for her editing of most of the chapters in this book and for her always appropriate observations.

Thank you to Dr. Jerry Mittelman for drawing the cartoon that appears in the beginning.

Thank you to the members of Interfaith Fellowship with whom I first shared many of these ideas. A fellowship may be defined as a mutual association of persons on equal and friendly terms, a communion, a companionship. The fellowship has been a true home of communion and companionship over the past several years.

Thank you to the readers of *On Course* magazine who first read most of these chapters as they were published in *On Course*. Thanks for your ongoing encouragement and support. My thanks to both the members of Interfaith Fellowship and to subscribers to *On Course*, who contributed enough money to buy the computer on which this book was written.

Thank you to Michael Leach, publisher and editor at Crossroad Publishing Co. for his encouraging words, his detailed reading of each chapter, and his suggestions for improvement.

Finally, my thanks to Dr. Kenneth Wapnick for his friendship of nearly twenty years, for his devotion to *A Course in Miracles*, for having consistently fostered my own growth and understanding of the *Course*, for his careful reading of this text, and for his suggestions for changes and improvement, many of which I have been able to incorporate in this work. I have not, however, incorporated all of Ken's suggestions, and I am sure he would not be in agreement with everything in this book.

The ideas represented here are the personal interpretation and understanding of the author and are not necessarily endorsed by the copyright holder of *A Course in Miracles*.

There was a man climbing alone in the mountains. He came to the edge of a precipice, looked over the side, felt vertigo, lost his balance, and fell.

Quickly he reached out and grabbed hold of a branch of a small tree. Suspended hundreds of feet in the air, unable to think of anything better, he cried out for someone to come to his rescue.

"Is anybody there?" There was a long silence.

Then a voice from absolutely nowhere said: "It's all right, my son. I'm here. I will take care of you. Let go."

There was another long silence and the man said: "Is anybody else there?"

Part I

Remembering What We Are By Forgiving What We're Not

Chapter 1

Introduction

A Course in Miracles is a self-study program of spiritual psychotherapy designed to help us remember God. We remember God as we undo our guilt through forgiveness.

Although the *Course* is set in a Christian context it deals with universal spiritual themes. The *Course* says that there are thousands of spiritual paths; the *Course* itself represents *just one way* of reaching Heaven. The focus of the *Course* is on the healing of relationships. As it says in the introduction:

> *"This course does not aim at teaching the meaning of love,*
> *for that is beyond what can be taught.*
> *It does aim, however,*
> *at removing the blocks*
> *to the awareness of love's presence."*
> —*A Course in Miracles*, Introduction

The *Course* consists of three books: a textbook, a workbook, and a manual for teachers.

1. *The Textbook* (669 pages) describes the theory of the *Course*.

2. *The Workbook* consists of 365 meditative exercises, one for each day for at least a year. You can spend several days on one exercise but should not try to do more than one exercise per day.

3. *The Manual for Teachers* (92 pages) provides a clarification of terms and addresses some often-asked questions, such as: How will the world end? and Is Reincarnation So?

A word about the references. The first edition of *A Course in Miracles* was published in 1976. Nearly one million copies of the first edition are in existence. The second edition was published in 1992 and contains minor corrections and revisions to the first edition along with the numbering of paragraphs and sentences. The first number following each quotation from the *Course* is the page number of the first edition. The second set of numbers, indicating chapter, paragraph, and verse, is for the second edition.

Quotations from *The Textbook* are noted with a T., from *The Workbook* with a W., and from the *The Manual for Teachers* with an M. An example for each book follows:

T.400; T-20.III.3:6

T.400	Textbook (1st ed.), page 400
T-20	Textbook (2d ed.), chapter 20
III	section III
3:6	paragraph 3, sentence 6

W.220; W-p.I.125.8:1

W.220	Workbook (1st ed.), page 220
W-p.I	Workbook (2d ed.), part I
125	lesson 125
8:1	paragraph 8, sentence 1

M.63; M-27.4:6

M.63	Manual (1st ed.), page 63
M-27	Manual (2d ed.), question 27
4:6	paragraph 4, sentence 6

Its Origin

The *Course* began in 1965 with Dr. Helen Schucman and Dr. William Thetford, both professors of medical psychology at Columbia University's College of Physicians and Surgeons in New York. Frustrated with the competitiveness and backbiting that so often characterize academic departments, Bill uncharacteristically turned to Helen one day and said, "There has to be another way." Just as uncharacteristically, Helen responded, "You're right — and I'll help you find it."

In this ground of joining in common purpose to heal relationships, the seeds for the *Course* found fertile soil and took root.

No doubt a genius, with a well-trained and rigorous analytic mind, Helen was also very intuitive, sensitive to her dreams, and receptive to visionary and mystical experiences. She had a keen ability to tune in to the needs of others. Helen's Jewish father described himself as an atheist. Helen's mother was for a time interested in Christian Science as well as a number of other approaches to spiritual life. She was also influenced by a Catholic nanny and a black Baptist housekeeper, both of whom introduced her to their religious traditions. Though attracted to the Catholic Church, Helen followed no particular religious path.

Shortly after turning to Bill and telling him she would help find a better way, Helen began hearing a voice, which she described as a kind of inner dictation, telling her to sit down and write. Being a rational-istic psychologist, she feared she was going crazy. One day the voice became particularly bothersome, and she called Bill to ask his advice. He suggested that it would not hurt to sit down and write and see what happened. The first line was: *"This is a course in miracles...."*

Details of Helen's life and the scribing of the *Course* can be found in Dr. Kenneth' Wapnick's book *Absence from Felicity*, published by the Foundation for *A Course in Miracles* in 1991. Another account is Robert Skutch's book *Journey without Distance*, published by the Foundation for Inner Peace in 1984.

The *Course* was published privately in 1976 by the Foundation for Inner Peace. Over one million copies are now in print, thousands of study groups have sprung up around the world, and conferences on the *Course* are now held throughout English-speaking countries. The Spanish edition was released in January 1993, and other translations are in progress.

The Voice of the *Course*

The *Course* is exciting because it works. It facilitates a positive change in perception enabling people to move from a fearful view of the world to looking at the world through eyes of loving forgiveness. Hundreds of thousands of people from all walks of life have found the *Course* meaningful.

The Voice in the *Course* is Jesus. If you believe that inspiration is something that happened, once and for all, a couple of thousand years ago or more, then you may not think this is possible. Yet it is clear that the Voice in the *Course* is Jesus. The author of the *Course* makes several references to his life as the historical Jesus of Nazareth.

One may also ask, Who is Jesus? Do we mean a historical figure who walked upon this earth and taught a group of followers some two thousand years ago? Yes, but is that all? From the standpoint of the *Course,* to talk about Jesus is to talk about something timeless, beyond the world of birth and death. To speak of Jesus is to speak of the Christ, the Son of God, the Self, that God created. To speak of the Self is also to speak of one's own True Self, which always has and will be a part of God.

This book is entitled *Awaken to Your Own Call* in keeping with the teaching of the *Course* that as we begin to awaken to the deeper call from within, we discover our True Self, which is part of Christ. The *Course* makes it clear that as we listen to the call from within we will be listening to ourselves.

> *"It is your voice to which you listen as He speaks to you."*
> —W.220; W-p.I.125.8:1

The purpose of the *Course* is to help us get in touch with the Christ, with our True Self, by learning to ask for and follow the instruction of the Holy Spirit, who is our Internal Teacher.

My Journey to the *Course*

My introduction to *A Course in Miracles* was foreshadowed by my experience as a farm boy in Missouri. There I was taken with a sense of nature mysticism that whet my appetite for religious experience. At the age of eighteen I began serving as a pastor of three rural Missouri churches (1961–64). During those same years, while in college, I made frequent retreats at a Trappist monastery near Dubuque, Iowa. During my time in seminary (1964–67), I became progressively fascinated with the study of world religions. When I was twenty-seven, I spent a month at a yoga ashram in Canada where, to my own surprise, I participated in a firewalking ceremony.

This firewalking experience so deepened my interest in yoga and Hinduism that in the summer of 1971 I took a backpacking trip through India, spending time with Sai Baba and Rajneesh. My last visit was with Muktananda. After several days in his ashram, I went into a cave to meditate. The cave, which was several feet underground, had no light and no sound. I sat down and said: "Am I supposed to stay here?" I had no more than asked that question when I thought I heard a "No!" followed by a rush of thoughts, all of which said: "Go back to New York. There you will find what you are looking for."

Back in the United States, I resumed an active career as a Methodist minister and professor at the New School for Social Research and New York University. At NYU I met Judith Skutch, who was teaching parapsychology there. Judy was a mover and shaker in the parapsychology community in New York City in the 1970s and she would frequently have friends over to meet Uri Geller or to see the latest in Kirlian Photography or other interesting developments.

In 1974 I wrote a letter that was published in the newsletter of the Association for Transpersonal Psychology. At the time I was working on a dissertation on the relationship between psychotherapy and spirituality, and my letter expressed interest in any relevant articles, books, or information from the transpersonal community. In January 1975 Bill Thetford saw my letter, and he and Dr. Ken Wapnick suggested to Helen that it was a call for her to complete scripting the pamphlet *Psychotherapy: Purpose, Process and Practice.* She had started the work earlier but never finished it.

Helen and Bill had heard me lecture a few years earlier at a Spiritual Frontiers Fellowship conference in the South. Helen remembered me and agreed that this was a call to complete the pamphlet. Helen completed the pamphlet in March 1975 and called to say that she had something she thought I would find helpful.

Helen invited me to meet her at Ken's apartment the following Sunday evening. At that time Ken was living in a small studio apartment on East 17th Street in New York City. I went to this meeting not really knowing what it was about. When I got there I met Helen, Bill, and Ken. Helen proceeded to tell me about *A Course in Miracles*, its development, and its effect on those in the room. By this time I had explored many different philosophies. Most of them had left me wanting something more. Though impressed with my colleagues,

I was concerned that I would again be left wanting. At the end of our meeting it was decided that Ken and I would get together for further conversations. I walked home that evening feeling that probably the most important thing that had ever happened to me had just occurred, but I was not sure what it was.

Shortly thereafter, in May of 1975, Helen met Judy Skutch. Judy and her husband, Bob Skutch, together with Helen, Bill, and Ken, were to start the Foundation for Inner Peace, which became the publishers for the *Course*. Judy began by having three hundred photocopies of the *Course* made and distributed, so a small group of us got an early start in studying the *Course*. The *Course* itself was printed and released in July 1976.

It was not until July 1976 that I really began to take the *Course* seriously. Doing so was precipitated by an event that I call my death experience. A few days after the experience I wrote a detailed description entitled *Holy Hell*, which I read to Ken, Helen, and Judy at Judy's apartment on Central Park West in New York City. It was clear to me from this experience that we are not our bodies, that we are making this world up, and that this is not the real world.

Memories of Helen

Ken and I became friends, and I sponsored several workshop with Ken as the leader (1977–84). Helen in turn became something of a mother figure, mentor, guide, and counselor in times of trouble — and it seemed I was frequently in trouble. I would meet Helen for counseling at Ken's apartment or at Judy's home, though never at her own apartment. She was always available by phone and was very supportive. She seemed intuitively to know when I was in trouble and would call to see how I was doing. Helen had an incredible ability to work with people in distress. At several points I felt frustrated with the Methodist church and called saying: "I've had it, I'm quitting." Helen repeatedly said she felt it important that I not quit, at least not then.

Helen was very direct and would tell me what to do in very clear terms. I was not, however, a good student and often resisted her advice. At one point she said I should let go of a relationship to which I was quite attached. I could not see how I could follow her advice and find peace. In this case, as in all others, she was right.

One of the most remarkable things about Helen was how she kept herself out of the spotlight when it came to the *Course*. Her name does not appear on the *Course*, and she avoided public lectures on the *Course*. Helen died in February 1981. At her funeral, Ken gave an eloquent eulogy in which he discussed Helen's devotion to God, but he never mentioned *A Course in Miracles*.

The Church and the *Course*

My favorite PBS series of all time was "The Ascent of Man" by Jacob Bronowski. I was particularly struck by the section on "The Starry Messenger," which discusses the life of Galileo. After Galileo invented the telescope, he was sure that he would be able to convince the world that Copernicus's theory was true — namely, that the sun and not the earth was the center of what was then the known universe.

It was clear to Galileo that what he saw in the sky stood open and revealed. The results did not at all please the church. Galileo thought that all he had to do was show that Copernicus was right and everyone would listen. Dr. Bronowski points out how naive Galileo was about people in authority.

Once I began to understand the *Course*, I was sure it would be just a matter of time before other ministers would start using this valuable guide in their ministry. I was sure that before long it would revolutionize the church. For fourteen years (1975–89) I tried to introduce the church to the *Course*. During this same period, while I was increasingly working from the *Course* and continuing to study and teach courses on the various mystical traditions and Eastern religions, the church became increasingly conservative. The next thing I knew there were fundamentalists in my parish complaining that I was not preaching the "saving grace of the blood of our crucified Lord Jesus Christ." It was true. I was not preaching sacrificial blood.

In June 1989 I left the Methodist Church, and in September 1989 Rev. Diane Berke and I started Interfaith Fellowship in New York City. A wholly new form of ministry became possible. Now in the

1990s, we've been able to actively and openly talk about the *Course* and watch its increasing popularity and acceptance.

I still believe that the *Course* will revolutionize the church by turning the focus from sin, guilt, and fear to love, forgiveness and, peace. I now realize that that change is going to come from lay seekers and clergy seekers alike who are rediscovering the heart of Christianity as expressed in the *Course*. *A Course in Miracles* may yet provide a Copernican revolution in Christianity because reality does not revolve around institutional systems of belief. It revolves around the truth.

A Course in Miracles is a philosophy of life that works for me as I know it does for hundreds of thousands of others. There are lots of ways of awakening. Still, there is but one mountain, one God — one peak experience. I may journey up the mountain from the west while you climb from the east. It makes no difference which side of the mountain we climb. We all begin from where we are. The more clearly each of us pursues our own unique path and the closer we get to the top, the more we realize how similar our paths have been.

It is the intention of this book to provide a way of understanding some of the basic teachings of the *Course*. It is in no way a substitute for the *Course* but may be helpful for those who are relatively new to the *Course* and are baffled by *Course* terminology. I also hope it will be helpful to *Course* students and others struggling to understand the sometimes difficult-to-grasp concepts that make up the *Course*'s metaphysical foundation and teachings.

We will begin by looking at the nature of the ego and the incredible systems of defense the ego uses to protect itself from what it perceives as threats to its existence. This includes the complex world of sin, guilt, and fear and the two primary systems of defense — denial and projection — as well as the particularly destructive form of projection we call anger.

We shall then turn to look at the practical application of the *Course* to our primary area of healing, namely, our interpersonal relationships, and to the primary means we have of healing relationships, namely, forgiveness. The *Course* understands forgiveness in a way very different from traditional Christianity. It is never a matter of making others wrong and then from a superior position seeking to forgive them; rather it is our task to remove all our projections of guilt onto others.

Then we shall turn to look at some of the metaphysics of miracles. Here we are dealing more with what sounds like a discovery of modern physics than one of traditional theology. There are several concepts in the *Course* that are unique to the *Course* — namely, that there is no world, no time, no devil, no hell, no body, and no death. These ideas seem particularly difficult to accept; nevertheless we shall try to understand what they mean.

Finally, we shall turn our attention to the Happy Dream — the dream of awakening — the realization that there is no love but God's and that we are able to awaken to our own call and return home again.

Chapter 2

Looking Better

"For now we see in a mirror dimly,
but then face to face;
now I know in part;
but then shall I know fully
even as also I am known."
—1 Corinthians 13:12

By the title "Looking Better" I do not mean that this is a discourse on how to be better looking, but on how to be better in our looking. The purpose of the *Course* is to help us look at the world from a spiritual perspective instead of an ego perspective. As we attain the inner peace that results from this change in perspective, we are able to share our peace with others and offer peace to the world.

In reading through the first several exercises in the *Workbook,* one of the things you notice is the importance placed on *seeing.* Among the first several exercises we find such statements as:

3. *"I do not understand anything I see."*

7. *"I see only the past."*

9. *"I see nothing as it is now."*

17. *"I see no neutral things."*

20. *"I am determined to see."*

21. *"I am determined to see differently."*

The Myth of the Ego

From the perspective of the *Course,* we do not really see anything as it is because our seeing is clouded by our ego-based thoughts. In fact, the *Course* points out, *"perception is interpretation."* The findings of modern physics, as well as the research of the Gestalt psychologists, verify that in perception the perceiver and the things perceived cannot truly be separated. What is perceived *is* inevitably influenced by the one perceiving. Perception is *inherently* interpretative.

Within the world of perception, the *Course* distinguishes two ways of seeing: that of the ego and that of the Holy Spirit, the Voice for God. Respectively, they represent the paths of:

Ego	or	**Holy Spirit**
Fear	or	Love
Hell	or	Heaven
Death	or	Life
Damnation	or	Forgiveness
Scarcity	or	Abundance
Time	or	Eternity
Sickness	or	Health
Pain	or	Joy

The perception of the Holy Spirit reflects Truth and the realm of knowledge, the Kingdom of Heaven, which the *Course* teaches is beyond the entire world of perception. What we need is the ability to come to what the *Course* calls the "Vision of Christ." With the Vision of Christ we begin to lay aside our judgment of the world and look upon the world with love. We need to be able to see everything as the Holy Spirit does, that is, as either an expression of love or a call for love.

In the context of the *Course,* the ego is a wrong-minded attempt to perceive ourselves as we wish to be rather than as we are. The ego was born out of the wish for separation and autonomy from God. The ego made time and fears for its survival because it knows not eternity. It does not know eternity because it is not itself eternal. This is why we fear death. In truth we cannot die, but the illusions we carry around with us about who we are can and will die or disappear.

Students of the *Course* often ask the question, How did the ego happen in the first place? A more helpful question is, Why do we continue to hold on to the idea of separation? Ultimately we cannot be separated from God. Ultimately there is no ego. As it is, however, we believe there is an ego and we believe it is possible to be separated from God. This belief, the *Course* teaches, is part of a dream, a fantasy that, ultimately speaking, contains no reality.

In this world, insofar as the ego "seems to exist," the ego is that which defines, describes, interprets, analyzes, condemns, projects, and judges. In one way or another, it is that which makes up the world. The ego is always making up the world. There are many different religions, many different belief systems. One is not right, another wrong. All are interpretations. All are wrong insofar as they are caught in fear and guilt and a fascination with the external. All have had a little taste of eternity. Problems arise when one system of belief says of itself that it is the only way to see things and others must conform to its interpretation. Consequently we have strife among different religions — even strife among different denominations.

Making Up the World

It is common knowledge in psychology that brain processes provide missing information or compensate for distortions in information. The mind makes up its own world.

> *"You make the world and then adjust to it,*
> *and it to you."*
> —T.400; T-20.III.3:6

A striking example of how the mind adjusts to the world it sees is shown in the work of experimental psychologist G. M. Stratton. Stratton made spectacles that turned the retinal images upside down. When he put on his glasses, he had trouble coordinating vision and movement, because he saw everything upside down and backward. After a week of living in an upside-down/backward world he began to adjust and eventually learned to walk, read, eat, write, and carry on his activities successfully. In fact, he eventually forgot he was living in an upside-down world. When he finally removed the spectacles, the world he saw was again upside down and backward, and he had to adjust all over again.

In the same way we make up our world, our society, and then live in conformity to it. We can't help doing this any more than we can avoid language or dialect or accent or culture.

> *"In solitude we have our dreams to ourselves,*
> *and in company we agree to dream in concert."*
> —Samuel Johnson, in *The Idler*

There are many ways in which illusions are developed and perpetuated. The more complex our world the more ways there are to sustain our dreaming.

A part of what I saw in my death experience and what the *Course* is telling us is that "we are making it up here." And we can make it up lots of different ways. The world we see is "merely a view," a construct, an attitude or way of seeing. We can choose to see the world the ego makes up and shows us — a world of sorrow, divisiveness, and sin — or we can choose to see the world the Holy Spirit offers us through the Vision of Christ — a world that reflects the healing, harmony, and happiness of God's love. The world the Holy Spirit offers us is a happy state of mind. It is not anything physical or observable. We live in fear and pain because we have not learned how to make choices with the Holy Spirit. We only know how to choose from the standpoint of the ego. But we can change and we can learn to see things a new way.

What Vision is Not

In order to understand what the *Course* means by true vision, or the Vision of Christ, it is helpful to look at what vision is not.

1. Vision is not physical sight

When the *Course* talks about physical sight, it is talking about the ego perspective. What our body's eyes see is misleading. For example, from a distance we see a man walking down the street and are sure it is our friend. We yell out his name, he turns around, and we discover we were wrong. Our perception has given us faulty information. Likewise, our interpretations and judgments, based on our fragmented egocentric point of view, are also faulty. In fact, we don't really see anything correctly as long as we look at the world through eyes shaded by the ego. "Ego glasses" show us the world the way we want to see it or the way we are making it up, rather than the way it really is.

There are, for example, many things in this world that we think of as valuable and important but contain no reality. The *Course* says that we are forever confusing form with content. It's not the form that matters; it's the content. Nothing in this world lasts. We place a great deal of importance upon physical beauty but it's certain that such beauty does not last. The form of things never holds eternal value.

True vision is a matter of *insight,* that is, the capacity to discern the true nature of our experience. Insight is an inward experience. To see the exterior world only, to see only bodies, physical and material things, is not vision.

2. True vision has nothing to do with judgment

> *"Vision would not be necessary*
> *had judgment not been made."*
> —T.412; T-20.VIII.1:5

True vision is actually the opposite of judgment. The ego makes a multitude of judgments about the world. True vision is not a matter of our determining what is right and wrong or good and bad. It is seeing things as they are, as part of God's eternal world. Judgment comes out of fear. Vision comes out of love.

> *"Judgment will always give you false direction,*
> *but vision shows you where to go."*
> —T.415; T-21.I.2:5

Vision reflects a decision *to accept* rather than *to judge.* It does not involve analysis or interpretation. It is instead the suspension of analysis and interpretation. Only as we suspend our analysis and interpretation can we have real clarity. Through the use of "justification" we can seemingly make the truth into a lie, and a lie into the truth.

3. Vision is not dreaming

> *"Vision is the means by which the Holy Spirit
> translates your nightmares into happy dreams."*
> —T.414; T-20.VIII.10:4

True vision has nothing to do with fearful dreams or nightmares. Nightmares are products of the ego. Only the ego can enter into fear and imagine itself cut off and separate from the whole. True vision has nothing to do with soap operas, movies, novels, illusions, pipe dreams, or fantasies. Our world is filled with all of these, which are merely distractions.

4. Vision is not wishful thinking, conjuring, hoping, or the use of positive affirmations

True vision is not discovering a parking space for ourselves and then saying that the Holy Spirit provided it for us. The mind is very powerful and can do all kinds of things, but they are not what the *Course* means by miracles. There is a story about a *Course* student who was on a diet. One morning on his way to work he decided to drive by his favorite donut shop. He told himself that if he saw a parking space, it would be a sign that the Holy Spirit wanted him to stop. Sure enough, the fifth time around the block there was a space right in front!

True vision does not require the use of affirmations to change the world or yourself. On subliminal tapes whom is the tape talking to — your ego or your real Self? We can say "I like myself" a thousand times a day, but if we do not truly *see* (know) our own purity and innocence, saying "I like myself" ten thousand times isn't going to help us like ourselves.

The Backward View

Though we feel something is amiss when we live within the framework of the ego, it never occurs to us that we are seeing things backward. The word "Ambulance" is written backward on the front of that emergency vehicle. When we read the word in the rear-view mirror, we see it as though it were written correctly. When we look in a mirror we see everything reversed, but it never occurs to us that everything is backward.

It is the purpose of the *Course* to help us understand that we have been looking at everything backward. We've been looking for the inside on the outside. The *Course* is here to help us look at things differently, to obtain a reflection of the inner reality rather than the outer illusion. To understand the inner life, we need a complete reversal in the way we look at things. We need to "do a 180." The following are a few examples of what it means to do a 180.

In this world we think that it is in taking that we receive. In the realm of the ego we are taught to "go for it," get it, make it ours. But why is it that once we get what we decided to go for, we still feel that something is missing? Something is missing because we attained only a little bit of this world. We didn't attain Heaven. We may have brought temporary satisfaction to our ego, but we're truly no richer than we were before. In fact we're impoverished until we are able to reverse our way of looking at things and see that it is not in taking that we get anything.

Truth is: It is only in giving that we receive.

In this world we think that by making judgments we are justified. If you listen to people talk, say at a coffee shop or on a talk show or at church, you will see how much time we spend in projection and in the reinforcing of mutual prejudices. One person will offer some thesis about what is wrong with the world, and another tops that illustration with an even better story to reinforce the same or yet another prejudicial point.

> *"The world you see*
> *is but the idle witness that you were right.*
> *This witness is insane.*
> *You trained it in its testimony,*
> *and as it gave it back to you,*
> *you listened and convinced yourself*
> *that what it saw was true."*
> —T.418; T-21.II.5:1-3

Truth is: It is only as we suspend judgment that we have an opportunity for clarity. We don't come to the truth by figuring it out. We come to the truth by becoming receptive to the Voice for God.

In this world we think that we are bodies. The cosmetics industry is a multibillion dollar industry; the medical industry is a multibillion dollar industry; the clothing industry is a multibillion dollar industry. Yet Jesus taught in his Sermon on the Mount:

> *"And why worry about clothing?*
> *Think of the flowers growing in the fields,*
> *they neither have to work or spin;*
> *yet, I assure you that not even Solomon in all his regalia*
> *was robed like one of these."*
> —Matthew 6:29

Truth is: We are not our bodies. Our fascination with our bodies keeps us from seeing. This is not to say we should do away with our bodies. This world is a classroom and our bodies are tools through which we learn. You cannot learn by dropping out of class.

In this world we think we can make ourselves right and in righteous indignation withhold our forgiveness. Yet:

Truth is: We experience love only by extending forgiveness.

In this world we think of everything in terms of past and future.

Truth is: The eternal now — this holy instant is the only time there is. Exercise No. 7 of the *Workbook* states: *"I see only the past."* It is because we see only the past that we do not see anything as it is. Jesus says we should *"let the dead bury the dead."* We cannot see anything clearly when our minds are preoccupied with guilt, regret, nostalgia, and remorse.

> *"If only I could take a potion*
> *that would enable me to forget."*
> —Swami Vivekananda

While our minds are focused on things of the past we are not really thinking. We are not thinking as long as our minds are caught in delusional thinking, which isn't *really* thinking. When we do something we are not very proud of, we often say that we just weren't thinking. To say that we were not thinking about a particular situation is to say that we lack vision. The whole task of the *Course* is to help us to look better; if we see only through the eyes of the ego we are not really seeing.

It takes courage to be willing to look at things differently and give up all our justifications. The ego does not want us to look clearly at our projections and our belief in guilt because, if we did, we might realize we do not want the ego's "gift." So the ego tells us we should be afraid to look and offers us the defense of denial and projection. The ego teaches that the guilt we cannot see or that we see in someone else instead of ourselves cannot hurt us. It does not tell us that not looking is the best way to hang on to guilt.

Looking is not easy because we do not want to admit to the fact that we have been seeing everything backward.

> *"One vision, clearly seen, that does not fit the picture*
> *as it was perceived before will change the world*
> *for eyes that learn to see...."*
> —T.615; T-31.VI.5:4

The Tiny Mad Idea

As long as we live with illusion, as long as we cannot see things the way they really are, we experience pain and imprisonment. According to the *Course*, however, beyond the limited sphere of our perception is a knowing without fault or flaw. This is Heaven. It is the pre-separated world of God and His unified creation. It is a space where there is no distinction between subject and object, where there is no pain and no fear. It is a space of pure love, a place where we already are in the mind of God. All else is illusion.

If we can look at the world with the Vision of Christ we will no longer see sin, sickness, and sadness. We will then understand that all such appearances reflect our belief in, and guilt over, what the *Course* calls *"the tiny mad idea"* that we have separated from our Source. If we had no guilt we would be able to look at the idea of separation and see how crazy it is. It is crazy to think that anything could destroy the love of God or change the perfection of what He created. At one point the *Course* says:

> *"It is a joke to think that time can come to circumvent eternity."*
> —T.544; T-27.VIII.6:5

It is the purpose of the *Course* to help us look at what we think of as our sinfulness and at the ugliness of what it calls our specialness — our desire to be singled out from the rest of creation and given special favor, special treatment, special love. With the help of God we can see that what we thought was so awful is not so awful — in fact it was nothing. It is awful only insofar as we believe it has the power to exclude God. If we can *look at* the ego with the Holy Spirit, we can no longer be caught in the ego. Our task is to be willing to be open to looking at things without attachment to the ego — without judgment.

If we can look at our ego without the perception of guilt and sin and recognize that we are afraid of love, then we can let it go. This is forgiveness. *A Course in Miracles* is not a course in magic. It is a course in miracles. It is a course in changing our perception. It is a course in undoing guilt through looking at it and seeing it in the light of forgiveness.

Switching Teachers

Forgiveness is not creating a problem in the first place. Forgiveness is letting go. Forgiveness is accepting. It is letting go of the ego's interpretation — the projection of guilt. Not looking at what the *Course* calls our *"special relationships"* is the way we keep them special (unhealed). Not looking at what we think is sin and guilt and fear is a way of holding on to our sin, guilt, and fear. It is by looking at it that we turn it over to the Holy Spirit. It is not looking at the ego that gives the ego power over us.

What is needed is light to shine away the darkness. We can't see anything if we are afraid to look. The *Course* simply asks us to look at things differently:

> instead of seeing ourselves as being betrayed,
>
> instead of thinking there is reason to be jealous,
>
> instead of thinking we can be hurt by someone's insult,
>
> simply to look at what we see without the attachment of our ego.

Our basic problem is that we have been relying upon the wrong teacher. Our task is to switch teachers. We have been relying upon the ego as our guide 99.9 percent of the time. But our ego (coming from fear) gets us nowhere. So our task is to switch guides. This does not require our doing anything other than being willing to set the ego aside. We are just asked to be willing to put our denial, our anger, our jealousy, our impatience, our judgment aside for a moment and look at it. We are simply asked to have the maturity to see these things in ourselves, look at them, and realize we do not need them. They are coming from the ego and do us no good.

The introduction to the *Course* tells us that the purpose of the *Course* is to help us *"remove the blocks to the awareness of love's presence."* All we really have to do is to be willing to look at the blocks that prevent true perception. We have to be willing to look at the blocks before we can put them aside. Then Christ's Vision can shine through. It's not up to us to decide what the Vision of Christ should show us. It is simply our task to be willing to look at our craziness. As Dr. Kenneth Wapnick has expressed it: "The purpose of the *Course* is not to help make this world a more loving place. The purpose of the *Course* is to help us look at this world in a more loving way." By doing this, we bring this world to healing and to love.

The Vision of Christ

When we see things the way they really are, without denial, projection, judgment, or condemnation, when we begin to come to the Vision of Christ, when we can just look upon the world without judging it, we can begin to truly see.

> *"See through the vision that is given you,*
> *for through Christ's vision He beholds Himself.*
> *And seeing what He is, He knows His Father."*
> —T.233; T-13.V.10:3

When we no longer look through the eyes of the ego, but see things instead from the viewpoint of our True Self, everything changes. There is no fear, for we cannot lose or be diminished in any way. Even death becomes nothing at all.

The famous preacher John Henry Jowett tells of visiting a cobbler in Wales and asking him if he felt cramped in his very small quarters.

"No," said the man.

He then told the preacher to follow him to a window that opened toward the sea. "When I feel tired and cramped, I look though that window and it steadies me."

The Holy Spirit opens for us a window that enables us to look to greater horizons. We need opportunities to Stop–Look–Listen, and see things without the clutter of the ego. Take a walk, go fishing, don't think about anything. What is really required is giving up our own attempt to make up the world.

True vision is knowing. When Martin Luther King, Jr., gave his famous "I Have a Dream" speech, he spoke from the realm of vision, not from the realm of dreaming. He told people about the good things that he saw, not as fantasies but as living realities. He held a vision that looked at things differently. He chose to look with the eyes of love instead of fear.

True vision enables us to see the Kingdom of Heaven reflected on earth — right here, right now. There is no need to wait for Heaven. Heaven is not something that is going to come someday. Heaven already is for those who see it.

True vision is the perception of the Holy Spirit that sees beyond the body to the spirit that is our true identity.

True vision sees forgiveness and sinlessness throughout the world.

As we drop our projections we see things the way Jesus saw them. It may happen first in a holy instant — in a moment of clarity in which we see some part of God's creation as it really is and are blessed by it.

True vision comes as we look upon someone or some situation we might have judged before and let it be what it is.

True vision is an experience of peace.

What Do You See?

It is possible to see a place where anger finds no home, where hurts are healed, a place that looks very much like Heaven. It is possible to see a place where loss is impossible, where love endures forever, where hatred cannot exist, and vengeance has no meaning. What would you like to see?

The next several chapters describe the processes by which we can begin to look at things differently.

Chapter 3

The Call Goes Unanswered

Now the word of the Lord came unto Jonah, the son of Amittai, say-
ing: "Arise, go to Nineveh, that great city, and cry against it; for their
wickedness is come up before me."
  But Jonah rose up to flee unto Tarshish from the presence of the
Lord and went down to Joppa; and he found a ship going to Tarshish;
so he paid the fare thereof and went down into it, to go with them
unto Tarshish from the presence of the Lord.
                                                           —Jonah 1:1–3

When we study hero mythology we notice that the hero or heroine invariably receives a call to undertake what becomes a life mission.

Jonah is called by God to deliver a message. Moses is called by God to deliver the people out of Egypt.

In *Star Wars* our hero Luke is called to save the princess Leah.

While the mission is often an external one it is also clearly internal. Not only must Moses save the people of Israel; he must, spiritually speaking, save himself in the process.

From the standpoint of the *Course* each of us is called to a higher mission; there is some task we are to perform. Our task is to remember ourselves, awaken to our own call, and come back home again. Yet this is a world of duality, where it is very easy for us to get caught in illusion, to forget our calling, and to see only a place of despair and imprisonment rather than a place of healing that leads us to an awareness of our true identity. Yet the fact remains:

"We have a mission here.
We did not come to reinforce
the madness that we once believed in."
—W.261; W-pI.139.9:1-2

Our mission is not to convert "lost souls." The mission is one of waking up, of remembering our true identity and returning home again. Yet in all hero stories the hero inevitably goes off course, gets caught in ego concerns, and wanders about seemingly lost.

I would like to share a short example of a hero myth called "The Hymn of the Pearl," a story from the *Acts of the Apostle Thomas*, written about the fourth century C.E. The following is my own abbreviated paraphrase of the hymn, a translation I made from the Greek when I was doing graduate studies some twenty years ago. The hymn is a story of a journey, of failure, of straying from one's purpose, of getting back on purpose and final victory.

The Hymn of the Pearl

There was once a young man who dwelt in a marvelous, rich kingdom and whose parents sent him out on a mission with provisions described as "great yet light," ones that he could carry alone. Before he left he removed his robe of glory and his splendid mantle. In his heart was inscribed a message concerning his destiny; he was to obtain a pearl that was lying in the middle of the sea encircled by a snorting serpent.

Making his way downward, he was accompanied by two royal envoys. The way was dangerous and hard and he was young. A stranger in the new world, he disguised himself in clothes similar to the clothes of those around him, and he kept to himself until he recognized another of his race, an "anointed one." They developed a trust in one another, and his friend warned him about the "unclean" ones. But the unclean ones, seeing that he was not a countryman, ingratiated themselves to him and mixed drink with cunning and gave him to eat of their meat, so he became progressively less aware of his mission.

His parents noticed all that befell him and wrote a letter calling him to awaken, to rise out of his sleep, to become aware of his bondage and remember his original mission. The letter came in the form of an eagle, which "became wholly speech." At its voice, he awoke and recalled in his heart the purpose of his journey.

He remembered that he was a king's Son, a "freeborn soul." He remembered the pearl and the snorting serpent. Going to the serpent, he charmed it to sleep by naming over it his Father's name. Seizing the pearl, he repaired for home, leaving behind his "impure garments." The voice of the letter now guided him with its light, encouraged his fears, and drew him homeward.

He had forgotten the "Robe of Glory" he had left behind in his childhood. Seeing it again, it became a mirror image of himself. "Myself entirely I saw in it, and it entirely I saw in myself." Now clothed in his robe, he ascended the gates of salutation and adored the splendor of his Father who had sent him and whose command he had now fulfilled.

This brief account of a hero's journey is your story and mine. We have been sent on a mission to a foreign land. This world is not our home. We now adopt the clothing (bodies) of this world, and having imbibed drinks mixed with cunning and getting caught in the dreaming of the world, we lose sight of our mission. Our task is to remember our mission and our identity, to fulfill our mission and return home again.

"There is no burden heavier than an unfulfilled potential"
—Charles Schultz

Why Don't We Respond to the Call?

In terms of the *Course* it is very easy to get caught in ego affairs manifest in terms of bodily, material, emotional, and psychological concerns. We get caught in fears and special relationships in which we find no peace, and it seems difficult for us to find our way home. The *Course* says the body is the ego's chosen home, and it is very easy to get caught up in the body.

Believing we are bodies we spend a great deal of time feeding and clothing the body and looking at our visage in the mirror. We are presented with a variety of possible addictions, alcohol, smoking, drugs, caffeine, fats and sugars. We perpetually seek bodily pleasures and try to avoid bodily pain. Sexuality seems particularly fascinating as it involves not only physical but also emotional and psychological pleasures. There is nothing wrong in any of these "things," but the minute we *have to have* something everything changes and we are no longer free.

Yet to attain the Kingdom of Heaven we must be burden free. Speaking of himself in the Gospels Jesus says that *"his burden is light, his yoke is easy"* because he had nothing to carry, to weigh him down. In addition to all of our physical concerns we are weighed down by emotional dependencies, our need to be liked, our need for self-esteem. Yet the message remains; we attain at last the Kingdom of Heaven only when we are burden free.

In *Pilgrim's Progress* the hero, Christian, begins his journey carrying on his back burdens with names like Fear, Envy, and Despair. He then goes through a variety of experiences like the Slough of Despond and the Valley of Humiliation. (Ever been to any of these places?) He learns something from each such experience and drops each of these burdens one by one until he reaches at last the Celestial City (the Kingdom of Heaven), as naked as Adam and completely unencumbered.

The Voice of the Ego / The Voice of the Holy Spirit

In every moment of every day we can listen to the voice of the ego or the voice of the Holy Spirit. The more we are caught in fear and ego concerns, the easier it is to be pulled off course and ignore the voice of God in our lives. Jonah does not do what he is called to do because he is afraid. To respond to God's voice and do what He wants us to do often seems too difficult. Like Jonah, you may hear the call and understand what you are supposed to do, but resist paying attention to the call.

We may even pretend that we do not hear the call, but the truth is that the Holy Spirit speaks to us every moment of every day. His voice, the *Course* says, is as loud as our willingness to listen. Once many years ago I was working as a leader of a therapy group, and there was a doctor and his wife in the group. The woman was seriously questioning her life and mission, feeling that her own life had been eclipsed by her husband's career. When I asked her to explain what she understood her mission to be she said that she did not know what it was. I pressed her, saying that I believe that in fact she did know and could tell us if she wanted to. Suddenly she stopped. She cried for a moment, and then said that she did know. She started speaking the truth as she had not done in a long time. Truth is, we all know what we are called to do if we just want to look at it.

> *"It is something very near to you,*
> *already in your mouth*
> *and in your heart;*
> *you have only to carry it out."*
> —Deuteronomy 30:14

Rather than paying attention we choose instead to become unconscious, get lost in our illusions and dreams, lose sight of our mission, and use our talents in service of the ego rather than our Higher Self. The result is frustration, anger, and despair.

This dark "slough of despondency" is nothing less than our ego's attack upon itself — an attack that will never work, though it may "appear" as though it will.

Moses, afraid to speak God's word, used his speech impediment as an excuse.

Jonah, unwilling to pay attention, wound up in the dark belly of a whale.

Each of us finds our own way to be neurotic — to put second-class things first and ignore the call within.

- Sometimes when we are most under attack by the ego, we may be the closest to a breakthrough.
- Sometimes when we are very far removed from the reality of this world, we are yet close to the real world.
- Sometimes when we are very far off course, then especially a transpersonal perspective is called for.
- Sometimes we have to be under a great deal of stress.
- Sometimes we need to break down and cry.
- Sometimes we need to admit to an ego attack.
- Sometimes we need to see things differently.

In the Belly of the Whale

In the midst of my disastrous attempt to own and operate a country inn and restaurant, suddenly one day things got completely unbearable. One dreadful rainy day I went up into the attic to check out the leaking roof. Looking up at the giant arching beams under the roof I suddenly felt like Jonah looking up at the ribs from the inside of this whale in which I had been swallowed. It was a particularly difficult day: the sewer was backing up, the mortgage holder was threatening foreclosure, and a tenant who was five months late in her rent was screaming that she was not going to make any payments until I made repairs — which I could not afford to make because she had not made any payments. Every time the phone rang it was somebody asking for money.

Suddenly, I had enough. I crawled out of the attic and went and sat at my desk and I prayed. I was in deep trouble and all I could say was "Help!" I said: "I'm not sure I'm good at praying but I need help." And then I had one of those rare experiences in which I actually thought I heard a comforting voice saying very simply: "Haven't I always taken care of you?" That was all I heard and all I needed to hear.

The *Course* says the voice of the Holy Spirit is always reassuring and will never frighten us. I didn't know what the solution was. But a new sense of peace came over me. Six months later like Jonah I was literally spit out of the mess. I lost nearly everything I had, financially speaking, but I was free. It was then that Diane and I started our ministry and began *On Course* magazine. I had to start over at the age of forty-six, but now at least I was paying attention. I was back "On Course" and doing what I had always been called to do.

Asking for Help

The resistance to paying attention and listening to the call of God in our lives can be very strong. Even though we are aware that we are off course, we don't seem to be able to stop our wandering. Instead, we choose to believe that if we continue to manipulate the world long enough, it will eventually give us what we want. Yet the constant process of trying to change the world is not what is called for. The real transformation can only happen within, which is why the *Course* tells us that *"we need do nothing."* All that is ultimately called for is a change of mind. Changing our behavior doesn't mean anything if the mind has not changed. Jesus says: *"As a man thinketh in his heart so is he."* Once the "within" changes, perception of the exterior changes as well. Suddenly the burdens, the addictions, the habits that seemed impossible to let go of are nothing at all, and we happily set them aside and go our way unencumbered.

I had been trying to make it on my own and now discovered that that was not necessary. When I finally responded and did what I was supposed to do, I found lots of people who wanted to help.

At any moment we can awaken to our own call. We can pay attention to the Voice that is calling us. We can respond if we want to. Making a first step back to God and toward the real goal can be as simple as a sincere request for help. As one of the old gospel hymns expresses it:

> *"Have you trials and temptations?*
> *Is there sorrow anywhere?*
> *Take it to the Lord in prayer."*

Sometimes that prayer need be nothing more complicated than a simple "Help!" Addicted to a drug, it may look as though you can never be free of it. Yet right now, this second, the decision can be made: "You don't have to." As Alcoholics Anonymous says it, take it "one day at a time" which means one minute at a time. "This minute, I don't have to."

> *"Never attempt to overlook your guilt*
> *before you ask the Holy Spirit's help.*
> *That is His function.*
> *Your part is only to offer Him a little willingness*
> *to let Him remove all fear and hatred,*
> *and to be forgiven."*
> —T.357; T-18.V.2:5

We Just Need a Little Willingness

We need to listen again and again. The destiny to which we are called is always there — always present — and it cannot be lost. The Holy Spirit's function is communication. As we bring the blocks that impede our progress to Him, His light shines upon us. It is thus that our fears are dispelled. The good news is that:

"Under each cornerstone of fear
on which you have erected your insane system of belief,
the truth lies hidden."
−T.267; T-14.VIII.2:7

We need to bring everything to the Holy Spirit, every secret we have ever locked away. There it will be undone and we can be free.

How Long Has This Been Going On?

Once the response is made, the results are wonderful. Actor Tony Randall tells of his discovery of opera at the age of thirty. He was taking voice lessons, and his teacher asked him to go listen to a particular male opera singer. Randall had always avoided opera, but now on the command of his teacher he went. He was enthralled. A new world opened up for him. At the end of the performance, he came out saying: "How long has this been going on?"

You can hear the call — for it is there. There is no need to live in bondage to anything — no physical addiction, no relationship addiction, nothing. There is nothing to do but God's will. Nothing else will ever make any of us happier. When we respond, when we do what God is asking us to do, we cannot but say: "How long has this been going on?" A treasure awaits each of us, not at the end of the rainbow but just inside the doorway of Heaven, very close to the Heart of Man.

Chapter 4

The Forgiveness of Sin

The idea of and belief in sin are central to the ego's thought system. From this central concept all other thoughts evolve, beginning with the belief in the reality of guilt, fear, and the need for punishment.

One Sunday a man went to church without his wife. When he returned home she asked him what the preacher talked about. He replied, "Sin." "Well" said the wife, "What did he have to say about it?" "He's against it," said the husband.

The church has always been against sin. As Billy Sunday, the famous evangelist in the early part of this century, expressed it:

> *"I'm against sin,*
> *I'll kick it as long as I've got a boot,*
> *and I'll fight it as long as I've got a fist.*
> *I'll butt it as long as I've got a head,*
> *and I'll bite it as long as I've got a tooth."*

Tell fundamentalists there is no sin, and they will tell you there is plenty of sin — all you have to do is to look around you. Furthermore, they say, if you say there is no sin then you'll just do whatever you want in the world without worrying about the consequences to others or yourself. The belief in sin is, they believe, necessary to keep us in line. This idea is based on a belief that our basic nature is evil and destructive, and thus needs to be controlled and held in check.

> *"There is no stone in all the ego's embattled citadel*
> *that is more heavily defended than the idea that sin is real."*
> —T.376; T-19.II.7:1

The Unholy Trinity

What is sin? Adam and Eve, having eaten of *"the fruit of the knowledge of good and evil,"* suddenly think of themselves as separate from, other than, God. This idea had never occurred before. They think of themselves as naked and seek to *"hide their shame."* God asks Adam why he is hiding, and Adam says that it is because he is naked. For the first time we have separation, we have a sense of sin, shame, and guilt. God wants to know where Adam got this idea of being naked. Adam blames what has happened on Eve. When God confronts Eve, she blames it on the serpent.

The ego now begins to build a system of defense. The ego is basically centered around three ideas on which it builds its defense, namely, sin, guilt, and fear. As Dr. Wapnick has pointed out: "This unholy trinity is a psychological hell and constitutes the ego" (*Forgiveness and Jesus,* p. 26). To understand the interweaving of these three ideas is to understand the structure of the ego.

The ego is the belief in the reality of the separated or false self, made as a substitute for the Self that God created. This use of the word "ego" is broader than the way the term is used in Freudian psychology, although similarities do exist, for example, with regard to ego defense mechanisms like denial and projection used as means of further backing into a sense of separation rather than moving toward God. However, the use of the word "ego" in the *Course* is actually closer to the use of the word in Hinduism and Buddhism

> *"A major tenet in the ego's insane religion*
> *is that sin is not error but truth...."*
> —T.375; T-19.II.4:1

Sin, or Missing the Point

The word "sin," as Jesus uses it in the New Testament, means *"missing the mark,"* or *"missing the point."* If we sin, we miss being centered in God. We are instead ego-centered.

Sin according to the *Course* is *"lack of love"* (T.9; T-1.IV.3:1). It is a mistake to be corrected rather than an evil to be punished. When we see the word "sin" in the *Course,* we can substitute the word "separation." Sin is the belief that we have separated ourselves from God and set up a self that is in opposition to our True Self. The Self in the *Course* is synonymous with Christ. Once we believe we are separate, it is impossible that we not feel guilty. Once we feel guilty, it is impossible for us not to fear punishment for what we think we have done.

From the standpoint of the *Course, sin is an illusion because the ego itself is an illusion.* It's not who we really are. We are not egos. Our reality is not as a frightened, vulnerable, mortal, separated self. What God creates must be like Himself, for His creation is the extension of His being. We are part of God, a thought in the Mind of God. This is not arrogance. It does not mean that we are God. But we are a part of God, as is Jesus.

> *"Yet where He is,*
> *there must be holiness as well as life.*
> *No attribute of His remains unshared by everything that lives.*
> *What lives is holy as Himself,*
> *because what shares His life is part of Holiness,*
> *and could no more be sinful than the sun could be made of ice;*
> *the sea elect to be apart from water,*
> *or the grass to grow with roots suspended in the air."*
> —W.287; W-pI.156.3:1-3

Once we do not see ourselves as separate, we can begin to let go of our identification with the ego and stop defending it. We can begin to give up denial and projection, live in the world just as it is, and see in it the reflection of God's beauty and love.

When Jesus intervened to prevent the stoning of the woman who had been taken in adultery, he demonstrated the principle of forgiveness by a loving God. When he said to the woman *"Go and sin no more,"* he was telling her, *"You are loved by God. Now, go and don't continue to miss the point. Don't continue to live in error, don't continue to distort and misperceive the reality of who you already are."*

Jesus did not condemn the woman for her error. He says: *"Neither do I condemn you."* It was the mob who condemned and demanded punishment. A loving Father does not condemn. God does not condemn. Because the ego cannot but judge, it condemns and then projects this condemnation onto God.

Management theory suggests two ways to manage. One is to focus on who is doing things wrong, who is goofing off, who is incompetent, and then either correct or get rid of them. In his best-selling book *The One Minute Manager*, Ken Blanchard explores another, more profitable method of management, namely, to catch people doing things right. You then support and encourage them to do even better. Not only is it a more effective way to manage; it's also more fun.

You can be for things or against things. But it's more fun to be for things than against them.

> *"If you attack error in another, you will hurt yourself.*
> *You cannot know your brother when you attack him."*
> —T.37; T-3.III.7:1-2

The *Course* asks us to look at who we really are, not as neurotic, projecting egos trapped in our own individual soap operas, but as the True Self that God created, as a son or daughter of God. This is not arrogance. It is the simple acceptance of our eternal reality rather than the limited view we might take of ourselves as egos. It acknowledges God, rather than ourselves, as our Creator.

Error or Truth

The problem with our usual thinking about sin is that we do not think of it as error, but as some truth about our being that cannot be corrected. To say that sin is not sin but error causes the ego to jump to the defense of the reality of sin. The idea of sin is sacrosanct to the ego's thought system and essential to the ego's existence.

> *"Any attempt to reinterpret sin as error*
> *is always indefensible to the ego.*
> *The idea of sin is wholly sacrosanct to its thought system*
> *and quite unapproachable except with reverence and awe.*
> *It is the most 'holy' concept in the ego's system."*
> —T.375; T-19.II.5:1-3

Saying that sin is an error in thinking or perception doesn't mean that we can justify or condone what we call sinful behavior. It simply says that such behavior is the inevitable outgrowth and expression of a false belief about our true identity and that of others. We have forgotten who we really are. We have misidentified ourselves as abandoned, unloved, unlovable, alone, and vulnerable. We have mistaken one another for enemies and thus justified unloving treatment of ourselves and each other. We have even tried to justify condemnation and cruelty in the name of righteousness and love. Since judgment, condemnation, and punishment only reinforce our mistaken beliefs, they cannot be a real solution to the problem.

To say there is no sin does not mean that we can do whatever we want in the world. The *Course* teaches that *"as we give so do we receive."* For every action there is a reaction. What goes around comes around. Thoughts are real things. Every thought has its effect. Obviously, then, we should be aware of what we are thinking. What is it we are projecting, what is it we are seeing?

The idea is to live free of error, not to continue to perpetuate error. We really begin to understand the *Course* only when we begin to put the *Course* into practice, when we begin to do what the *Course* asks of us, as we lay our prejudice aside, as we relinquish our anger, as we realize that our jealousy is of our own making and gets us nowhere. Then it is that our so-called sins can no longer have any affect upon us because we have not chosen to perpetuate error.

Once we no longer perpetuate error we are free (no longer obsessed or possessed) by something that did not become us in the first place—because it wasn't us. To awaken to our own call is to awaken to who we really are, not as some sniffling, whining little ego caught in illusions, but as a son or daughter of God. As a son or daughter of God we cannot err. It is literally unthinkable.

Search out the devil and what do you find?

Search out the Kingdom of Heaven and what do you find?

Chapter 5

It's Not Your Fault!
Understanding Our Guilt

*"Perhaps some of our concepts will become clearer
and more personally meaningful
if the ego's use of guilt is clarified."*
−T.77; T-5.V.1:1

We need a clarification about guilt because we spend a great deal of our time wallowing in it and don't seem to be able to find our way out of it. There is no one who has not or is not now struggling with guilt as a major issue in life.

What Is Guilt?

- Guilt is the experience of having separated ourselves from God and thereby having attacked God.

- Guilt is the psychological experience of the belief in sin, the experience of having done something wrong.

- Guilt is self-hatred, a feeling of inferiority and incompleteness.

- Guilt is manifest in our sense of failure, apathy, and despair.

- Guilt is experienced as a basic feeling of the "wrongness" of our being.

- Guilt is a sense of shame about our bodies.

- Guilt is always disruptive.

- Guilt is more than merely not of God. It is the symbol of attack on God.

Problems in relationships according to the *Course* are always projections of guilt. Rather than looking at the guilt within, we find it more convenient to see guilt in the other. Because of guilt, special relationships have elements of fear in them (T.291; T-15.V.4:1).

> *"Guilt is the psychological experience of this belief in sin and can be defined as the total of all our negative thoughts, feelings and beliefs about ourselves."*
> —Dr. Ken and Gloria Wapnick,
> *Awaken from the Dream,* p. 83

Before the onset of guilt Adam and Eve lived in the present, in the now. They had no sense of finitude, nor fear of death. God was taking care of them. As with a fetus in a womb, everything was taken care of. As there was no sense of separation there was only peace, abundance, well-being, freedom, innocence, and joy.

Much of our guilt is associated with our bodily life. The *Course* says that the body is the ego's chosen home. It is obviously a place of separation. Adam and Eve seek to cover up their nakedness and hide their guilt by tying fig leaves around themselves. Still today, we associate shame with certain bodily functions and avoid having private parts exposed "for shame." The clothing and cosmetic industries capitalize on our need to cover up and adorn the body to make it more attractive — thereby emphasizing the importance of the body.

Each of us can think of many things we have felt guilty about. There is no one among us who has not lied, who has not been thoughtless or condemning of others. Each of us has been selfish, pushy, arrogant, and rude. Each of us has had the occasion to lose our tempers. We have cheated at a game or in school or on our taxes.

> *"Guilt is the only need the ego has, and as long as you identify with it, guilt will remain attractive to you."*
> —T.297; T-15.VII.10:4

Much of our guilt is unconscious. Like an iceberg with most of its mass beneath the water, our guilt is hidden beneath our conscious awareness. It is precisely because our feelings of guilt are so deep that we think we cannot overcome them.

Enter Fear and the Belief in Punishment

The ultimate source of our guilt is the belief that we have sinned against God and that the ego-self is our reality. Believing we have done something wrong and harmful to God, we inevitably believe we will be punished for our sins. A basic difference between traditional Christianity and the *Course* is in understanding how to handle guilt. Traditional Christianity says the guilty should be punished. I once heard a minister say that there must be a hell and sinners must go there — otherwise "it just wouldn't be fair."

Webster's Dictionary defines "guilty" as "deserving of punishment." Once we think we are going to be punished for our sin we become afraid.

> *"Only the fearful can be egotistic."*
> —T.77; T-5.V.1:3

Adam and Eve hide because they fear God will retaliate and punish them for their transgression, even though God had never been anything but loving toward them. This is the basic dynamic of the ego. Believing it is guilty, it projects its guilt onto God as anger and then fears punishment. Projecting our fear and guilt onto God transforms our experience of a loving, caring Father into a God who is wrathful and punitive. Consequently, we read in the Old Testament statements like *"Vengeance is mine, sayeth the Lord," "I will visit the sins of the fathers unto the third and fourth generation,"* and *"The wicked shall perish."*

Because we fear God, when we are anxious and need help God is not the one we turn to. We turn instead to the ego. The ego, fearing God, makes the experience of God's love inaccessible. This reinforces and increases our experience of separation, sin, guilt, and fear. We become more and more certain that God is not going to help us or will actively punish us. Associated with our sense of guilt is our belief in scarcity. Fear dominates our thoughts and lives — "I might get sick"; "I won't have enough money to pay the bills"; "I'm going to die." Freedom, abundance, wholeness, and eternity are impossible for a mind filled with fear.

When we self-righteously or angrily say to someone else, "May God forgive you your sins," we are clearly not saying, "There is an eternally loving Father who but awaits your remembrance and return to Him." Rather we are seeking to deny our own experience of separation and guilt by projecting it and making it real in the other — reinforcing the reality of sin and separation. From the standpoint of the *Course,* God cannot forgive sin because God never condemned in the first place. Condemnation is of the ego, not of God.

> *"Ask not to be forgiven,*
> *for this has already been accomplished.*
> *Ask rather, to learn how to forgive,*
> *and to restore what always was to your unforgiving mind...*
> *You will feel guilty till you learn this."*
> —T.260; T-14.IV.3:4-5, 8

Fear has often been used as a motivator, but we cannot come to God in fear. Fear may lead to compliance, but it also breeds resentment and hatred. Whenever we attack someone or try to frighten someone into doing what we want that person to do, we only increase defensiveness and resistance. If we promote fear in the name of love, we obscure the reality and truth of love behind dark clouds of confusion. Punishment and fear do not undo sin. Because they are part of the system of the ego, they simply reinforce and perpetuate one another. Understanding sin as "error" calls not for punishment but for correction of perception.

Correction

In truth, we cannot separate ourselves from God. We can only believe we have done so, and then experience this belief as our reality. We can misperceive reality and, like the prodigal son, live in a nightmarish world of our own making, seemingly far away and cut off from home. But just as the father never condemned the prodigal son, never sent him away or punished him, God has not condemned us. It is our belief in the reality of our separation that keeps us living in "the far country" of misery, pain, guilt, and fear. From the standpoint of the ego the Atonement is the process of "expiating," or paying for, our sins by and through punishment.

We need to remember that:

"In Heaven there is no guilt, . . . and
what is truly blessed is incapable of giving rise to guilt. . . . "
—T.77; T-5.V.2:1, 3

How Do We Overcome Guilt?

We cannot get rid of guilt by ritual practice, by fasting, sacrifices, and giving away our money. We cannot get rid of guilt by putting on sackcloth and sitting in ashes. The correction for guilt is simply not to deny or project it but to have the courage to look at it and begin to allow for the process of forgiveness to work through us.

" . . . the first step in the undoing
is to recognize that you actively decided wrongly,
but can as actively decide otherwise.
Be very firm with yourself in this,
and keep yourself fully aware that the undoing process,
which does not come from you,
is nevertheless within you because God placed it there.
Your part is merely to return your thinking
to the point at which the error was made,
and give it over to the Atonement."
—T.83; T-5.VIII.6:3-5

All problems are correctable. Correction involves understanding the conditions that gave rise to the problem and changing the misperceptions that underlie those conditions. If sin is an error in our mind, then correction occurs by changing our minds — by looking at ourselves and the world another way. All expressions of "sin" — disease, hatred, war, physical or emotional abuse of all kinds — can be corrected if we can correct the mistakes in our minds. This is the real meaning of healing.

We all can deceive ourselves. But ultimately we cannot, no matter how much or how long we might try, deceive God. The ego's fantasy is that it can create its own world, apart from God. As long as we accept this world of illusion as real, we may think of ourselves and others as sinful, separate, and guilty. God has not separated Himself from us. It is we who separate ourselves from Him. But this is not permanent or eternal. Since it takes place only within the illusory world of time and the ego, it is not real. Like the prodigal son, we can return home any time.

> "... your guilt arises from your failure
> to fulfill your function in God's Mind...."
> —T.260; T-14.IV.3:9

> "All real pleasure comes from doing God's Will."
> —T.12; T-1.VII.1:4

The *Course* asks us to exchange our perception of sin for the perception of error and innocence. As we joyfully release others from our perception of sin, we can all live in peace.

The *Course* suggests saying the following to ourselves whenever we feel guilty and afraid, remembering that the Holy Spirit will respond fully to our slightest invitation:

> "I must have decided wrongly
> because I am not at peace.
> I made the decision myself,
> but I can also decide otherwise.
> I want to decide otherwise,
> because I want to be at peace.
> I do not feel guilty,
> because the Holy Spirit will undo all the consequences
> of my wrong decision if I will let Him.
> I choose to let Him,
> by allowing Him to decide for God for me."
> —T.83; T-5.VII.6:7-11

Chapter 6

Freedom from Fear

"There is no fear in love,
but perfect love casts out fear.
For fear has to do with punishment,
and he who fears is not perfected in love."
—1 John 4:18

The Path of Love and Fear

The *Course* says that fear and love are the only emotions of which we are capable. Actually, it is only love of which we are capable on the deepest level, for love is of God. Fear is an emotion arising from the ego, which ultimately exists not at all.

Fear, not hate, is the opposite of love. Fear is the emotion of the ego just as love is the emotion given us by God. Think of a time when you were most fearful and you can probably see that you were very much in your ego. Think of a time when love filled your heart and you can see that you also felt close to God.

Just as sin and guilt go together, so does guilt walk hand in hand with fear — for fear is generated in the thought that God will castigate us and punish us for our sins.

"The attraction of guilt produces fear of love,
for love would never look on guilt at all.
It is the nature of love to look only upon the truth,
for there it sees itself,

58

with which it would unite in holy union and completion.
As love must look past fear,
so must fear see love not.
For love contains the end of guilt,
as surely as fear depends on it."
—T.382; T-19.IV.A.i.10:3-4

As we go through life the road ahead often divides and we have to choose to follow the lead of God or the ego. With each decision we make, we choose once again between love and fear, sanity and insanity, Heaven and hell.

Ann Landers says that of the more than fifteen thousand letters she receives each month, the problem most often reported is fear. The letters tell her that people are afraid of losing their health, their wealth, their loved ones.

Teaching Fear

Fear has its origin in the guilt we feel over the separation we think we have established between ourselves and God. Believing we have attacked God by opposing Him, we are afraid He will attack us in return. Fear arises when what we want conflicts with what we do.

"Whenever there is fear,
it is because you have not made up your mind."
—T.26; T-2.VI.5:8

We want to be honest, but we are dishonest "for fear." When we fear punishment, it is difficult to remember God's love. When we are afraid, we cannot see love, even when it comes our way. While love is one, fear is a fragmenting emotion. Fear is manifest as anxiety, worry, depression, and phobias. It tears us apart and reigns in madness, seeking to replace love.

Fear is the foundation on which all neurosis, psychosis, fighting, wars and the building of all systems of defense are based. We built our huge arsenal of nuclear arms — "for fear" of what the Russians might do to us. They built their arsenal — "for fear" of what we might do them. Fear causes people to do terrible things, as we see, for example, in the story of the young boy with AIDS whose home was burned by neighbors who were afraid of him. Many black men and women in the last century, and the early part of this one, were lynched for fear. Throughout the ages, millions of such stories have been told.

"Fear is insatiable,
consuming everything its eyes behold,
seeing itself in everything,
compelled to turn upon itself and to destroy."
—W.298; W-pI.161.7:5

"Mistake not the intensity of rage
projected fear must spawn."
—W.298; W-pI.161.8:3

The church has often taught sin, guilt, and fear in order to "scare" us into being good. But are you really good if your proper behavior comes from fear? Teaching fear as a means of bringing about correction only perpetuates misperception. Nowhere may this be better understood than in the murdering of murderers as a means of stopping murder. Teaching fear only creates further separation. It cannot bring about correction of misperception.

One day I was sitting at a booth in a diner. Sitting at another booth was an older man with his back to me. Across from him were two very young children — perhaps seven and eight years old. Suddenly the man began scolding the children in a loud voice. The other patrons of the diner and I established eye contact, and there was a growing sense that someone should intervene. From where I was sitting I could see the fear-ridden faces of the children, who were recoiling into the corner of the booth. I could also see the sense of separation. They were powerless at that moment, but you could tell that someday, as soon as they could, they were going to get away from that man.

The *Course* says that the purpose of fear is to conceal love. So the presence of fear should be understood as a call for love. Its presence shows us that we have written a fearful script — a script we could relinquish. Fear is an experience outside of eternity. It is always fear of something that might be — not what is. Fear is a time-based experience. Love is eternal.

Finding Freedom from Fear

The *Course* tells us that the mind is very powerful. It is up to us to decide whether we are going to turn the mind over to the ego — in which case it can play out silly, fearful, soap-opera games — or we can decide for God. Jesus is our elder brother. He serves as an example of someone who repeatedly chose love instead of fear.

"It was only my decision
that gave me all power in Heaven and earth.
My only gift to you
is to help you make the same decision."
—T.71; T-5.II.9:2-3

By deciding for God, Jesus showed us that the decision for God can be made. We can make it. Whatever we believe in becomes real for us. If we see ourselves separated from God we affirm the reality of separation. We cannot, therefore, experience God's love. What we need is a correction of this misperception. There is only one place and one way in which this correction can occur. It must occur within the mind.

"Whenever you are afraid,
it is a sure sign that you have allowed your mind to miscreate
and have not allowed me to guide it.
When you are fearful, you have chosen wrongly.
You must change your mind, not your behavior,
and this is a matter of willingness. . . .
Correction belongs only
at the level where change is possible."
—T.25; T-2.VI.2:10, 3:2, 4, 6

Real change can occur only at the level of mind. We may change our behavior but that does not mean that we have changed. If we change our mind, then change on the behavioral level follows automatically, and will be a real change. A change will thus have occurred at the level of cause, not at the level of symptom.

"The correction of fear is your responsibility.
When you ask for release from fear,

you are implying that it is not.
You should ask, instead,
for help in the conditions
that have brought the fear about.
These conditions always entail
a willingness to be separate."
—T.25; T-2.VI.4:1-4

Fear cannot be real without a cause. God is the only cause of everything that is real. All else is illusion. For this reason, there is nothing to fear — not even death or the end of the world. Ultimately, everything rests in the arms of God. Though there are passages calling for the fear of God in the Old Testament, God is not the author of fear. What is really being called for is respect for God — which calls for the relinquishing of our egos in favor of guidance from Holy Spirit. The ego is the author of fear, and if there is one thing we are not, it is our egos.

A Dream of Fear and Love

I would like to share a dream I had a long time ago. It was one of those vivid dreams that stays with you. It said more about how love overcomes fear than mere words could ever do.

In the dream I was with two other young men. We were walking and came upon a peninsula with an amusement park on it. On the edge of the park was a tunnel, like a tunnel of love — only this was the *tunnel of fear*. One of the young men was particularly anxious to show us the inside of the tunnel. Though the other young man was very resistant to going through the tunnel, for some reason the two of them went through while I walked around on the outside. When they came at out the other end, the hair of the fellow who had been resistant had turned white. He fell on the ground in a fit, foaming at the mouth.

After a while, the young man recovered and my companions proceeded further onto the peninsula, but I decided to stay behind. I climbed into the top of the tunnel through an attic or loft-like door, much like the one on our barn when I was a boy. It was my intention to expose the inside of this place and show that it was just machinery that had caused my friend to become so fearful.

When I entered the loft, I found that indeed the place was filled with demonic creatures, just as one would see in a book on demonology. I looked at them and proceeded to walk into the room. As I did, they started to back away respectfully. I realized that as long as I was not afraid they were powerless over me. For some reason, however, I was not afraid and kept moving forward. They kept moving back. Finally I stopped, and one of the larger and more human-looking ones approached me. She asked me if I would like to see the devil himself. I said I would, and she led me into a side room.

The devil himself was a little boy sitting in an aluminum lawn chair, with his arms resting regally on the arms of the chair and his head bent down to his chest as though he were pouting about something. I walked over to him, knelt down beside him, put my arms around him and said, "I love you. I love you." As I said that he began to shake violently and started to scream "No. No. You can't say that!" And puff! he disappeared like so much gas. At that very instant, I awoke.

The dream was a clear reminder that in the presence of love, fear is absolutely powerless.

There Really Is Nothing to Be Afraid Of

When we are afraid we need to remember: *Now* is the time to call upon the assistance of the Holy Spirit. As long as we do not protect fear, the Holy Spirit can reinterpret it for us. To do this is to help bring about a miracle. The correction of fear is always our responsibility — because we must let go of our fear for the Holy Spirit to take over.

Teach no one to be afraid of you. Teach no one that you are afraid of them. Do not be afraid to look upon fear, for it cannot be seen. Even in what we might perceive as a frightening situation, awareness of who we are and what our function is can keep us safe.

Several years ago there was a well-known television circus show that included a Bengal tiger act. Like the rest of the show, it was done "live" before a large audience. One evening the tiger trainer went into the cage with several tigers for a routine performance. The door was locked behind him. The spotlights highlighted the cage, the television cameras moved in close, and the audience watched in suspense as the trainer skillfully put the tigers through their paces.

Suddenly, in the middle of the performance, the lights went out! For twenty or thirty long, dark seconds the trainer was locked in with the tigers. In the darkness they could see him, but he could not see them.

When the lights came back on he calmly finished the performance. In an interview afterward, he was asked how he had felt during the blackout, knowing that the tigers could see him but he could not see them. He admitted that it had been a tense situation, but, he said: *the tigers did not know he could not see them.* He simply kept talking to them until the lights came back on.

When we are afraid, it is helpful to keep talking to that which would frighten us and remember that as long as we do not give in to our fears they are powerless over us.

The *Course* says that only the sane can look upon stark insanity and raving madness with pity and compassion but not with fear (T.393; T-19.IV.D.i.11:2). It is only when fear is shared that we give it reality. Because the trainer had no fear of the tigers, the tigers remained powerless over the trainer.

The *Course* assures us that Love is the only possible eternal state. As children of God we are all ultimately taken care of. We already are being taken care of; we just don't see it.

Whenever we are fearful we need to recognize that:

- Somehow we have made a wrong choice; we have chosen for the ego instead of God.

- As we have made a wrong choice, it is possible to choose once again.

The *Course* says that those whom we do not forgive we fear (T.393; T-19.IV.9), and that we cannot attain to love while fear still resides within our hearts. As long as we are unwilling to forgive anyone we will fear that person.

An act of forgiveness will help to correct misperception. Fear is of the ego, and the ego isn't real. That which is real is realizable. Fear has nothing to do with God's Kingdom. Freedom from fear occurs as we accept the Atonement for ourselves, realize that our sins were of the ego's making, and learn that the ego is not who we are. Only that which is of God is eternal. Everything else is part of a dream.

The ego came into time. The ego will disappear in time. It is possible to be freed of the whole entangled mess of sin, guilt, and fear. What's wrong in this world is not something that is in need of our anger and attack. We need only correction of our own perception.

The only whole and eternal state is love. God is love. We are here to teach only love. In love's presence fear cannot abide. As fear and love are the only alternatives for us, when fear has gone, love must take its place.

> *"If you knew Who walks beside you*
> *on the way that you have chosen,*
> *fear would be impossible."*
> —T.353; T-18.III.3:2

Chapter 7

Getting Off De Fense:
Removing the Blocks to an Awareness
of Love's Presence

On the first page of *A Course in Miracles* it says that the purpose of the *Course* is to help us:

> *"remove the blocks to the awareness of love's presence."*

Defenses are blocks. As we become aware of these blocks and realize that we do not need them, we learn to let them go. As we let them go we must inevitably awaken more and more to our own call.

> *"Defenses are the costliest of all the prices*
> *which the ego would exact.*
> *In them lies madness in a form so grim that hope of sanity*
> *seems but to be an idle dream, beyond the possible."*
> —W.277; W-pI.153.4:1-2

Most of us are so well defended, using defenses so unconsciously and frequently and with such ease, that we are not even aware of the fact that we are using them. All defenses are ways of keeping the truth from being whole. They are all ways for us to ignore our responsibility.

In order to change things we need some conscious awareness of what is going on. Without awareness of why we behave the way we do, we just drift in an unconscious haze and life never really gets better.

While there are many forms of ego defenses, the most important are denial and projection. In this section we'll begin by looking at defenses as a whole and try to understand what they are, why we use them, and what are some of the most common forms of defense — what in psychology are called *"first-line defenses."* Next we'll move to a study of denial, then to projection, and then to the destructive form of projection that we call anger. We'll conclude by looking at the Atonement as a defense.

The story is told of a Hassidic Rabbi named Zussya, who said that when he came before the throne of God he was concerned, not that God would ask him why he was not more like Moses or Abraham or Jesus, but rather why had he not been more like Zussya?

Why are any of us not who we could be? Why are we not doing what we could to fulfill our own personal destinies? Why do we create hell for ourselves and others when we could be moving toward the Kingdom of Heaven?

The hidden agenda for each of us is to become ourselves, to do what we came here to do, to get out of the painful illusion of thinking that we are something other than who we truly are as sons and daughters of God. The ego gets caught in time. Being caught and fearing for its survival, it creates defenses to protect it from the outside world.

Systems of Defense

Defense mechanisms are techniques we use to either distort or exclude from conscious awareness the source of the anxiety we feel, in order to make it less anxiety-producing. A defense is a device we use to "protect" ourselves from guilt, fear, and seeming attack from others. Defenses actually do the opposite of what they intend to do. Rather than making us feel more secure, the use of the defense increases our sense of guilt and therefore the separation we feel between ourselves and God. By definition defenses increase our sense of vulnerability: if we were not vulnerable, why would we need defenses? By using defenses, rather than removing our guilt we actually increase our fear and reinforce the belief that we need defenses. The result is a round of increasing defenses with no relief in sight.

> *"And herein lies the folly of defense;*
> *it gives illusions full reality,*
> *and then attempts to handle them as real.*
> *It adds illusions to illusions,*
> *thus making correction doubly difficult."*
> — W.245; W-pI.135.1:2, 3

Defenses are totally unnecessary, yet we create the defense *"for fear"* that if we did not we would be vulnerable. As a child of God our invulnerability has been guaranteed, but if we are not aware of our reality as children of God, then we may see ourselves as weak and frail and in need of defense. Even the youngest infant begins to display the use of defenses when it has unpleasant encounters in the world. The first cry as we come out of the womb is a defense.

A clear example of complex systems of defense is, of course, the military defenses developed by the United States and the now-defunct Soviet Union. These are really expressions of the ego out of bounds. During the past several decades the United States and the Soviet Union each spent billions of dollars on defense. Each country went deep into debt to pay for a defense system, each feeling it necessary to protect itself from the other. Yet as each side built up more weapons, the overall level of fear grew rather than decreased. Now we see that the defenses were not necessary, and each is faced with a huge debt that seems impossible to pay.

Ego defense mechanisms are "schemes" we use to conceal anxiety from ourselves and the world. A defense is a kind of magic wand we wave to protect ourselves when we feel threatened.

> *"Consider what the ego wants defense for.*
> *Always to justify what goes against the truth,*
> *flies in the face of reason and makes no sense."*
> —T.446; T-22.V.2:1-2

All defense mechanisms share three characteristics:

- They distort (falsify) reality.

- They usually operate in such a way that we are not fully aware of what is taking place. In other words, they all involve some kind of hiding—from ourselves, from others, and from God.

- They keep us from fulfilling our destiny and becoming more aware of God's Kingdom.

Sometimes we are very aware of our lies, pretenses, and protective maneuvers. But defenses become so automatic and easily triggered that we are not usually aware of their presence. We lie, hide, and pretend with incredible ease. The "quick-forgetting" of the part we play in making our own reality makes our defenses seem beyond our control (W.245; W-pI.135). Husbands and wives, parents and children, throw out a host of jabs and attacks that simply make others more defensive.

As we begin to grow spiritually, we begin to "unravel" our defenses in order to see more clearly, to become a part of God's Kingdom — a space of consciousness where there are no defenses.

First-Line Defenses

Defenses, rather than helping us make our way through the world, are actually inhibitors to spiritual growth. Defenses keep us from getting close to others and maintain our separation from God. Sigmund Freud aptly explored and exposed a host of ego defense mechanisms. Psychologists have described four lines of defense, ranging from the most common and least destructive to the most harmful.

As an army might send out certain waves of defenses — first bombardment by air, then bombardment with big guns, then the tanks, and finally the foot soldiers — so do each of us have lines of defense. We start out with the simplest, easiest, and closest at hand, like lying. We lie to "protect ourselves" from what we see as a threat. There is only one reason why we would ever lie and that is because we are afraid. If we were not afraid we simply would not lie. There would be no need for it.

Not all defense mechanisms are "entirely" harmful. Nevertheless, we need to be aware of them so we can begin to unravel or drop the need for their use. First-line defenses begin with our conscious efforts at maintaining control through manipulating the environment.

1. Removing ourselves from sources of stress

This system is quite common; it is the first one we learn as we encounter difficulties as infants. Psychologists have noticed that distressed children will inevitably "turn away" from the source of distress. A man irritated with work conditions may quit his job and find a less stressful situation. The dissolution of a relationship may happen for similar reasons. Sometimes it is necessary to remove ourselves from the source of stress in order to gain perspective. Of course, we cannot walk away from every frustrating job, nor can we move away from every relationship in which we feel frustration.

2. Sublimation

Freud felt that sublimation was a positive defense. Sublimation is a form of displacement or the diversion of emotional energy from its original source. But in this case the energy is used constructively. In *Civilization and Its Discontents* (1930) Freud suggested that Leonardo da Vinci's urge to paint Madonnas was a sublimated expression of his longing for reunion with his mother, from whom he had been separated at an early age. In fact, Freud thought that civilization itself rested on the sublimation of our sexual and aggressive impulses.

3. Extroversion or the directing of one's interests to phenomena outside oneself

Extroversion is a form of ignoring our real duties by devoting ourselves to hobbies, recreation, and social activities. Some diversions may lead to better health (physical activity), or more wealth (hobbies that are income-producing). Overindulgence in any activity may, of course, be a means of avoiding responsibility. For example, a husband and father may ignore his responsibility to his family by dedicating himself to golf, racing cars, or boating.

4. Workaholism

> "... a nation rushing hastily to and fro,
> busily employed in idleness."
> —Phaedrus ca. 20 C.E.

Workaholism often goes unnoticed, as it appears "productive." Yet it can be used to avoid the inner life. Busy earning a living, we don't have time to live.

> *"Life is what happens to you*
> *while you are making other plans."*
> —John Lennon

By staying busy we can ignore what's really going on. Then, as in the parable of the man who built bigger barns, our life story is over and we wonder what it was about. There has been no time for rest, reflection, meditation, and the discovery of the inner life.

5. Indulging in fantasies and daydreaming

> *"Yet it is certain that you will never find satisfaction in fantasy,*
> *so that your only hope is to change your mind about reality."*
> —T. 158; T-9.IV.10:2

It's not engaging in fantasies or daydreams per se that is destructive; it's indulging to the point of neglect of our responsibility that turns it into a problem. We live in an age where the average family watches TV seven hours each day, and with all the movies at the video store escapism is more readily available than ever before.

6. Rationalization, or providing logical justification for behavior motivated by inner need

"I did it because...." By rationalizing we give ourselves a plausible explanation for doing (or not doing) something. We may ignore the homeless man on the street who asks for money by saying that he would only spend the money on liquor. This allows us to avoid the feeling of guilt that we might experience if we thought we were refusing a deserving person.

7. Use of philosophic credos

Similar to rationalization is the adoption of codes of behavior and ethics to reinforce our conscience or to justify indulging our impulses.

- "Might makes right."
- "America, love it or leave it."
- "An eye for an eye and a tooth for a tooth."

8. Emotional indifference or apathy

For each of us there probably have been many times when we simply felt that we "could not get involved," when the stresses and anxiety of another were more than we cared to acknowledge or help with.

9. Escaping into bodily satisfaction, such as overeating or sexual indulgence

> *"The stomach is the greatest of the deities."*
> —Euripides

> *"The stomach is the reason*
> *man does not mistake himself for a God."*
> —Friedrich Nietzsche

Because as we cannot live without eating and because as it is a pleasurable activity, it's easy to fall into eating as an addiction. To relieve stress almost everyone has at times escaped into eating or sexual activity.

10. Alcohol, drugs, and other chemical and emotional indulgences

The use of such defenses are particularly unconscious and can lead to physical and emotional addiction.

•

To live in the Kingdom of Heaven means to live free, defenseless lives. We do many things in this world to avoid truth and our responsibility — to continue to hide our real identity from ourselves and perpetuate the illusions of the ego-self. It's helpful to become aware of even our simple defenses. We need to be more conscious of the degree to which we use them and notice the inhibitive role they play in our lives. What are the things you would hide or defend? Do you lie? Is it really necessary, or is truth-speaking also possible?

The world itself provides no safety. Yet safety is always possible in the arms of God. When we recognize our true identity, we see that we are safe and there is nothing from which we need protection. When we feel the need arise to be defensive about anything, we have identified ourselves with an illusion.

Defenses of any sort are ways of avoiding. Defenses, conscious or unconscious, cause us to feel guilty — for we know we are not paying attention to the truth but are choosing to ignore the truth in favor of some lesser distraction.

We need no defense because we have been created unassailable. Defenselessness is required for the truth to dawn upon our minds with certainty (W.248; W-pI.135.21:3).

As we become more aware of our defenses we can begin to lay them aside. The next time you start to lie or defend yourself in any way, "catch yourself and stop it." See if you cannot speak the truth instead.

The less we use defenses the more authentic life can be. To be defenseless is to remember our true identity as children of God.

"In my defenselessness my safety lies."
—W.277; W-pI.153

Chapter 8

Making Believe

Jesus said to them, "You will all fall away; for it is written, 'I will strike the shepherd, and the sheep will be scattered.'

"...After I am raised up, I will go before you to Galilee."

Peter said to him, "Even though they all fall away, I will not."

Jesus said to him, "Truly, I say to you, this very night, before the cock crows twice, you will deny me three times."

But he said vehemently, "If I must die with you, I will not deny you." And they all said the same.

...As Peter was below in the courtyard, one of the maids of the high priest came; seeing Peter warming himself, she looked at him and said, "You also were with the Nazarene, Jesus."

He denied it, saying, "I neither know nor understand what you mean." And he went out into the gateway.

The maid saw him, and began again to say to the bystanders, "This man is one of them."

But again he denied it. And after a little while again the bystanders said to Peter, "Certainly you are one of them; for you are a Galilean."

But he began to invoke a curse on himself and to swear, "I do not know this man of whom you speak."

And immediately the cock crowed a second time. And Peter remembered how Jesus had said to him, "Before the cock crows twice, you will deny me three times."

And he broke down and wept.

—Mark 14:27–31, 66–72

Denial of the Truth: Repression and Concealment

The fundamental defense mechanism that keeps threatening thoughts and memories from consciousness by pushing them out of our awareness is denial.

"The ego exerts maximal vigilance
about what it permits into awareness."
—T.59; T-4.V.1:3

In Goethe's *Faust*, the devil identifies himself by saying:

"I am the spirit of denial."

Repression was one of Freud's earliest discoveries. Freud observed that without considerable probing his patients were unable to recall traumatic or psychologically damaging childhood events. Traumatic memories, he said, were concealed from awareness by strong forces. Freud and the *Course* are in agreement at this point, namely, that our propensity for denial is very strong.

"Denial has no power in itself,
but you can give it the power of your mind,
whose power is without limit.
If you use it to deny reality,
reality is gone for you."
—T.118; T-7.VII1:5, 6

Freud felt that when unpleasant memories were very strong it was necessary for us to expend considerable energy to conceal them from others and ourselves. Freud felt that the anxiety generated in this process of concealment was the basis of neuroses and psychoses.

One day, as Linus and Charlie Brown were walking along chatting, Linus said,

"I don't like to face problems head on.
I think the best way to solve problems is to avoid them.
In fact, this is a distinct philosophy of mine.
No problem is so big or so complicated
that it cannot be run away from."

We start gaining weight and pretend we are not. We spend too much and try to ignore the debt. Each of us may notice symptomatic expressions of denial in our normal physical or emotional functioning, in things like sleepiness, disturbed memory, emotional indifference, and apathy. I once knew a woman who slept through most of the day every Saturday, convinced that she needed a full day of sleep to overcome the pressures of the previous week.

No one likes to be confronted with what they perceive as unpleasant aspects of their personalities. We don't even like to be told that we "might" be mistaken. Who likes to be confronted with overeating or extravagance? Confront an alcoholic about his alcoholism and you will run into considerable denial. No real change or freedom is possible until that individual is able to admit that, in fact, things have become unmanageable.

Sweep It under the Carpet

According to the *Course*, by repressing, denying, or putting out of our minds matters that really need our attention we keep ourselves from awareness of our true identity. We use these defenses as an excuse for inappropriate behavior: "I couldn't help it. I didn't know." "I wasn't there when it happened." It's been said that when we do something inhuman we excuse ourselves by saying: "After all, I'm only human."

When a simpler first-line defense like lying doesn't work, we go to the ego and look for help and the ego gives us a further lesson in irresponsibility by saying: "Push it aside. Make believe it is not there. Deny it, repress it. Forget it. Put it out of your mind."

When in our fear we use denial of the truth, as Peter did, we put ourselves in an unhappy position. If something is upsetting us and we are not fulfilling our destinies, we can ignore the whole thing by "pretending" we just cannot find our true destiny. Of course this does not make the problem go away. Denial might be thought of as "selective forgetting" or "selective remembering." We remember what we want, or what we can deal with, and forget the rest.

One of the ways we typically deny the reality of God and the truth of our identity is by becoming obsessed with lesser issues — what Dr. Ken Wapnick calls pseudo-problems.

> *"By becoming involved with tangential issues,*
> *it [the ego] hopes to hide the real question*
> *and keep it out of mind.*
> *The ego's characteristic busy-ness*
> *with nonessentials is for precisely that purpose.*
> *Preoccupation with problems set up to be incapable of solution*
> *are favorite ego devices for impeding learning progress."*
> —T.61; T-4.V.6:4-6

We can hide and pretend, we can bury our heads in ostrich-like fashion, we can busy ourselves with lesser things, but eventually we are going to have to look at the truth. The problem with denial is that the repressed material is really not forgotten and continues to gnaw away at our psyche. Like a cavity in a bad tooth, it slowly works its way toward the nerve. Eventually, whatever we are hiding must be acknowledged. As Jesus said:

> *"There is nothing hidden that shall not be revealed."*

Examples of Denial

Gail Sheehy in *Pathfinders* tells the story of a depressed woman faced with a mid-life crisis who consistently refused to acknowledge her unhappy marriage. She eventually got out of her depression only by admitting to herself and others that the situation was, in fact, not okay and that she needed help.

A man intent upon becoming wealthy may choose to ignore the deleterious effects his ardent pursuit is having on his family. We may completely forget to pay a bill for some extravagance. We may forget to do a job that seems noxious to us. We may forget an appointment with the dentist. We easily "overlook" things that would cause us discomfort.

Psychologists have given names to some of the major forms of denial.

Reaction formation, or the replacement of an anxiety-producing impulse by its opposite

The purpose of reaction formation is to make a person unaware of the original source of distress. Someone afraid of his or her own impulse toward homosexuality may express hatred of homosexuals. Crusaders who "protest too much" against what they see as reprehensible behavior often repress their own feelings or impulses by projecting them onto others. Those bent on exposing sins and waging "holy wars" against "evildoers" conveniently overlook the fact that they are going against the teachings of Jesus. Generally the stronger the impulse toward socially unacceptable behavior, the stronger the defense against it.

Displacement

With displacement an impulse or feeling is redirected to a different, less threatening person than the one to whom it is really directed. A man who is angry at his boss but is unable to do anything about it yells at his wife instead. Children are often the unfortunate recipients of displaced anger. Displacement can become a phobic reaction — that is, a profound, irrational fear of certain things such as snakes or spiders.

Regardless of the form of our denial, our primary denial is the denial of God.

> *"Allegiance to the denial of God is the ego's religion."*
> —T.176; T-10.V.3:1

The ego is afraid to admit the reality of God for fear of its own destruction. If the ego were to admit the existence of God, then it must deny its own reality. Therefore the ego will not allow for the awareness of God. What we fail to recognize in this process is that the denial of God is the denial of our own true Identity.

Denial of Illusions: Correction

The *Course* also speaks of a positive use of denial, namely, the denial of illusions.

The Bible speaks of *"the peace of God which passeth understanding."* This peace is totally incapable of being shaken by errors of any kind. It denies the ability of anything not of God to affect you. This is the proper use of denial. It is not used to hide anything, but to correct error. It brings all error into the light, and since error and darkness are the same, it corrects error automatically.

> *"True denial is a powerful protective device.*
> *You can and should deny any belief that error can hurt you.*
> *This kind of denial is not a concealment but a correction.*
> *Your right mind depends on it.*
> *Denial of error is a strong defense of truth,*
> *but denial of truth results in miscreation,*
> *the projections of the ego.*
> *In the service of the right mind the denial of error frees the mind,*
> *and re-establishes the freedom of the will.*
> *When the will is really free, it cannot miscreate,*
> *because it recognizes only truth."*
> —T.16; T-2.II.2:1-7

Each of us has denied and repressed more than we are willing to admit. When we were children each of us had experiences we would rather not remember. Recognizing and accepting some of the seemingly bad things — not judging them, just letting them be and seeing that they were in fact a part of the illusions of our egos, we can let them go and move a long way toward an awareness of who we really are as sons and daughters of God.

> *"When a situation has been dedicated wholly to truth,*
> *peace is inevitable."*
> —T.371; T.19.I.1:1

Chapter 9

There Is No "They"

"Judge not, that you be not judged. For with the judgment you pronounce you will be judged, and the measure you give will be the measure you get.

"Why do you see the speck that is in your brother's eye, but do not notice the log that is in your own eye?

"Or how can you say to your brother, 'Let me take the speck out of your eye,' when there is a log in your own eye?

"You hypocrite, first take the log out of your own eye, and then you will see clearly how to take the speck out of your brother's eye."
—Matthew 7:1–5

In the spring of 1992 I was teaching a class on religion at Mercy College. Although I usually teach in prison, this was an evening course on campus and the majority of the students were adults who had returned to college to complete their degrees. It was the next to the last class, and we were reviewing for the final. Having completed the review we still had about twenty minutes of class time left, so I asked the class what they would like to talk about.

The acquittal in the Rodney King beating case had just been handed down, and violence had broken out in Los Angeles. So the natural topic for discussion was race relations and violence. The students were all white except for one Indian woman. I let them voice different opinions about the problem. In short order a dispute broke out between the "prejudiced" and the "non-prejudiced" students, though it was sometimes difficult to see who was on what side. Tension began to rise in the room. What I could not help but notice in this conversation was the repeated use of the pronoun "they."

Somehow the problem was seen as somebody's fault and the solution to the problem was perceived as the responsibility of George Bush: "He should send in the troops." Or the problem was seen as the fault of the justice system, or the states, or corrupt police, or the parents, or religion. There was soon so much projecting going on in the classroom and so much use of the word "they" that I had to intervene and tried to suggest another way of looking at the situation. It wasn't easy, however, as many student now sat with folded arms, each convinced of their "rightness" and the others' "wrongness."

First, Remove the Log

When first-line ego defenses fail and the ego cannot successfully put something out of the mind through denial or repression, the next line of defense is projection.

The defenses of denial and projection go hand in hand. Both attempt to disguise guilt. Denial hides our guilt inside; projection throws guilt outside. When we deny, we simply suppress or repress guilt by pushing it into our subconscious. Projection reinterprets our guilt, telling us that what seems to be our guilt really belongs to someone else, so we blame someone else in order to escape blaming ourselves.

Projection is the process of ascribing to others one's own ideas and impulses. When we project we take our problem and say, "The problem is not in me. It is in you." Etymologically the word "projection" means "to hurl away." We choose someone or some group whom we can make responsible for how bad we feel. We then separate ourselves from them either literally or psychologically. We place distance between ourselves and them, then say that they are the ones who are cold and judgmental. We then feel justified in attacking them for whatever we have projected onto them.

A man or woman who is tired of a relationship may break it off, claiming that the other is no longer committed.

"In running away from ourselves,
we either fall on our neighbor's shoulder
or fly at his throat."
—Eric Hoffer, *The True Believer*

In Matthew 7, Jesus is speaking to those of us who would fly at our neighbor's throat rather than falling on our neighbor's shoulder. He makes it clear that all forms of attack are based on misperception. He tells us to turn the other cheek. He tells Peter to put away his sword. As we give, so do we receive. As we attack, so do we experience being attacked.

"Projection and attack are inevitably related,
because projection is always a means of justifying attack.
Anger without projection is impossible."
—T.89; T-6.II.3:5-6

Attacking increases our sense of guilt. Though ostensibly aimed at the outside world, attack inevitably winds up as attack against ourselves, for we cannot but feel guilt for our projections. We feel worse, and so does the person we have attacked.

Projection Makes Perception
"The world you see is what you gave it
and nothing more than that.
As a man thinketh, so does he perceive.
Therefore seek not to change the world
but choose to change your mind about the world....
Damnation is your judgment on yourself,
and this you will project upon the world.
See it as damned,
and all you see is what you did to hurt the Son of God.
If you behold disaster and catastrophe,
you tried to crucify him.
If you see holiness and hope,
you joined the Will of God to set him free."
—T.415; T-21.Intro. 1:1, 2, 6, 7; 2:1-4

From the ego's point of view, the object of our projection doesn't matter. We often project onto the one closest to us. For this reason we find many abused wives, children, and husbands. We attack whomever seems to be most immediately responsible for the unpleasantness we feel — whoever has left the dirty dishes in the sink, anyone else who has not fulfilled some responsibility.

When God catches up with Adam and Eve in the Garden, Adam says, *"Eve made me do it."* Then God looks at Eve, who says, *"The serpent [devil] made me do it."* Projection stands at the very beginning of the ego's development.

Favorite Choices for Projection

1. The devil made me do it

Among religionists, the all-purpose scapegoat is the devil. Blaming the difficulties we encounter in life on the devil keeps us from acknowledging our own mistakes. In acknowledging our shadow, we begin to see that the devil is not something to be destroyed but to be forgiven and undone. The devil is a construct of the ego, the symbol of all that is wrong in the world. The devil is that onto which we push our guilt and fear. He is our projection. He has no power. The devil is, in fact, nothing. He holds no "eternal" reality. As long as we project onto the devil, however, it looks as though he has lots of power.

2. Blaming it on God

If we don't blame it on the devil, a second easy choice is God. I once had a friend who was involved in an automobile accident. She was convinced that God was at fault for not having prevented it. She was driving too fast and not wearing a seat belt, yet in her mind it was God's fault.

3. The sins of the fathers

Freud taught us that our parents messed us up, so we blame them. But who messed them up? What about the doctors, the scientists, the government, the priests, or the schoolteachers. Maybe the real culprit is the neighborhood pharmacist. It used to be the communists.

"The basic difference between capitalism and communism
is that under capitalism man exploits man,
and under communism it's the other way around."
—John Kenneth Galbraith

Large institutions are easy prey for our projections, as are their leaders. It's difficult to understand why anyone would want to be president, knowing how much the president is the target of projection. Presidents are assassinated, the pope is shot, civil rights activists are slain, all out of someone's fearful projection. Iraq projects onto the United States and the United States projects onto Iraq.

Counseling often fails just when real change is possible. Just as we reach the point of looking at our projections, we become frightened and stop looking. A forty-five-year-old patient of Dr. Carl Jung once blurted out, "But I could never admit to myself that I've wasted the best twenty-five years of my life!"

It takes courage to accept responsibility for our projections. As we stop projecting we begin to see our own responsibility in whatever is happening. Whatever we see out there is part of our own psyche in need of healing and forgiveness.

"If you can imagine someone
who is brave enough to withdraw all his projections,
you get an individual who is aware
of a considerable shadow.
Such a man can no longer say
"they" do this or "they" must be fought against.
Such a man knows that whatever is wrong in the world
is in himself
and if he only learns to deal with his own shadow,
he is doing something real for the world.
He has succeeded in shouldering
at least an infinitesimal part
of the gigantic unsolved social problem of our day."
—C. G. Jung, *Man and His Symbols*

The more separation we feel, the more we may think others are out to get us. The more persecuted we feel, the less we acknowledge that we have anything to do with our feelings.

"Projection means anger,
anger fosters assault,
assault promotes fear."
—T.85; T-6.I.3:3

Assault can be made only on a body. You are not a body. One body can assault another, but that has nothing to do with who anyone is as a child of God. This is the message of Jesus on the cross. All kinds of projections were being placed on him. He had become the scapegoat of the Romans and the Pharisees. Yet he was aware of the truth. He knew who he was despite what anyone else said. They could kill his body, but it meant nothing. The Son of God, the perfect Self that God created, cannot be killed. The eternal is not affected by the temporal.

Whenever we choose to see ourselves as persecuted, we fail to assume responsibility for our own life. You cannot project and tell the truth at the same time. Admitting to a mistake in perception opens the door for greater perception. Whatever unhappiness any of us are now experiencing cannot be blamed on God or the devil, our parents, our children, our husband, wife, or lover, the United States government, our boss or our employees.

Not blaming anyone outside ourselves for our unhappiness does not mean that we should blame ourselves. Blaming is faultfinding and calls for judgment, condemnation, and punishment. Blame reinforces separation. When we blame ourselves, we reinforce our own experience of separation and guilt. Taking responsibility simply means recognizing that what is called for is a change, a correction — in thinking, in perception, in attitude. What is called for is love and along with it healing through forgiveness.

Extension, the Right Form of Projection

Just as there is a correct form of denial — namely, the denial of error — so too is there a right-minded attitude with which we can use our capacity to project or, to use *Course* terms, extend.

"We have learned, however,
that there is an alternative to projection.

Every ability of the ego has a better use,
because its abilities are directed by the mind,
which has a better Voice.
The Holy Spirit extends and the ego projects.
As their goals are opposed, so is the result."
—T.89; T-6.II.4:1-4

We can extend healing instead of hurt, comfort instead of pain, love instead of fear. We can extend what the *Course* calls the happy dream in place of a nightmare. Then it is that we begin to see the world as whole, healthy, and worthy of love.

When we judge others, we do not know what circumstances stand behind their behavior. The Sioux Indians have a saying that you should not judge another unless you have walked a day in that person's moccasins. Every now and then I like to quote an old poem from what I call "homespun American philosophy." The following anonymous poem reflects the need for us to suspend judgment, for we never know what another has gone through:

"Pray don't find fault with a man who limps
Or stumbles along the road,
Unless you have worn the shoes he wears
Or struggled beneath his load.
There may be a tack in his shoe that hurts,
Though hidden away from view,
Or the burden he bears, placed on your back,
Might cause you to stumble too.
Don't sneer at the man who is down today,
Unless you have felt the blow
That caused his fall, or felt the same
That only the fallen know.
You may be strong, but still the blows
That were his, if dealt to you
In the selfsame way at the selfsame time,
Might cause you to stagger, too.
Don't be too harsh with a man who errs,
Or pelt him with words or stones,
Unless you are sure, yea, doubly sure,
That you have not errors of your own.

For you know, perhaps,
if the tempter's [ego's] voice
Should whisper as soft to you
As it did to him when he went astray
'Twould cause you to falter, too."

Chapter 10

Anger Is Never Justified

He was still speaking when Judas, one of the twelve, appeared and with him a large number of men armed with swords and clubs, sent by the chief priests and elders of the people.

Now Judas had arranged a sign with them. "The one I kiss," he said, "he is the man. Seize him."

So he went up to Jesus and said, "Greetings, Rabbi," and kissed him.

Jesus said to him, "My friend, do what you are here for." Then they came forward, seized Jesus and took him in charge.

At that, one of the followers of Jesus grasped his sword and drew it; he struck out at the high priest's servant, and cut off his ear.

Then Jesus said to him, "Put your sword back, for all who draw the sword will die by the sword."

—Matthew 26:47–52

"Respiration deepens:
the heart beats more rapidly; the arterial pressure rises;
blood shifts from the stomach and intestines to the heart,
central nervous system and the muscles;
the processes of the alimentary canal cease;
sugar is freed from the reserves in the liver;
the spleen contracts and discharges its contents
of concentrated corpuscles, and adrenaline is released."

—Dr. Walter Cannon,
professor of psychosomatic medicine,
Harvard University

The proceeding statement, as you no doubt guessed, is a description of anger's effect upon the body. When it comes to its effects on our psychic system it's even more baffling. As an irate customer once said in response to a payment reminder: "You've made me so think, I can't mad straight."

The defense mechanism of projection takes on many forms. Projection is first a thought. When expressed, the thought is "thrown out" into the world, where it has its effect. The *Course* says there is no thought that is without its effect. A spoken thought often has its effect in very direct and immediate ways. A clenched fist or actual physical attack obviously has a very clear effect.

> *"Projection and attack are inevitably related,*
> *because projection is always a means of justifying attack.*
> *Anger without projection is impossible.*
> *The ego uses projection only to destroy your perception*
> *of both yourself and your brothers."*
> —T.89; T-6.II.3:5-7

To be angry, we must first think that we have been violated in some way, and according to the *Course* anger always involves projection of separation.

The word "anger" originally meant "the pain or smart of a sore or swelling." When we "accidentally" hurt ourselves, the first response is often to curse and damn the situation. A hurt ego's immediate response is often to make others pay for what they have done — to make them regret it.

While none of us may ever want to get angry, we do. The *Course* says anger is "never justified." Never. That certainly doesn't mean it isn't going to come up. It doesn't mean we should never be angry. If it happens, it happens. If it happens, we need to look at it.

Anger and Guilt

According to the *Course* anger is always an attempt to make someone feel guilty. No matter how cleverly disguised, anger is always an attempt to justify to the other person, ourselves, and the world the projection of guilt. It is a way of saying: "You are the sinner. You should feel guilty. You should change so I don't have to."

> *"Anger is an acid*
> *that can do more harm to the vessel in which it is stored*
> *than anything on which it is poured."*
> —Anonymous

Rather than correcting misperception anger increases defensiveness. Instead of making the other person feel guilty, we make the other increasingly defensive and ourselves more guilty. If we were enlightened beings, when our brother or sister got angry with us we would be able to handle it. As we are not enlightened, we often respond in anger; the situation is further aggravated and the sense of separation increases.

Paradoxically, the more we project our guilt the more we hang on to it. There was a man in Texas who had $45,000 stolen by a couple of swindlers. He got so mad he spent three years and $300,000 tracking down the men who had stolen the $45,000.

Maestro Toscanini would sometimes get so ferocious with his orchestra that he would throw anything in sight. One day he reached into his pocket and, snatched his very expensive pocket watch, and threw it on the floor, smashing it beyond repair.

Understanding Anger

According to the *Course* whenever we project we attack. Whenever we attack, get angry, or even annoyed, we feel guilty because we know inside that we are attacking unjustly.

Once when I was in college I drove up to Chicago during spring break to visit one of my college friends. While I was there my car began to give me trouble. My friend's brother tried to fix it but wound up making it worse than before, rendering it inoperable. I remember projecting my anger onto this young man and, even while I was doing so, feeling guilty. He had really tried to help, and it was not entirely his fault that the situation was now worse. My actions did not, of course, sit well with my friend. Though I later apologized, things were not quite right between us from then on.

Anger occurs because we believe we have been attacked. Believing we have been attacked, we can find justification for attacking in return. Thus we project away from ourselves the idea that we are responsible for our anger. It does not matter what others have done or what we think they have done. We attack to get rid of our own guilt. Otherwise we would not do it. The guiltier we feel, the more we need to attack. The more we attack, the guiltier we feel.

> *"An angry man is again angry with himself*
> *when he returns to reason."*
> —Publicus Syrus

Round and round we go on a spiral of increasing complexity, a spiral of depression and the sense of isolation we create between ourselves and others.

Ignorance and Anger

> *"Fear always springs from ignorance."*
> —Ralph Waldo Emerson,
> in the *American Scholar*

When we talk about anger we are talking about ignorance or a lack of awareness. Because we are not enlightened beings we do not have awareness — just perception. We perceive, we respond. Because we are ignorant, that is, lacking in knowledge, we choose for the ego instead of for God.

> *"An angry man opens his mouth*
> *and shuts up his own eyes."*
> —Cato

Buddha's great enlightenment was that "the whole of life is desiring." Desiring or attachment causes misery and suffering. To see where our desires and attachments are is to see the complexes of our lives — the places where we are hung up. A hang-up is the place we are caught, where we are hooked. It's the thought or addiction we cannot let go.

Notice where, when, and about what you get angry. Around that object of anger there is some place you are attached. Perhaps you expect another human being to behave in a certain way, and when that person does not, you get angry.

The cause of desiring, Buddha said, was ignorance. Jesus says the same thing. There is no need to make judgments about ignorance. We need rather to engage in our own spiritual education and purification.

The *Course* says there is no such thing as unforgivable sin. That does not mean that we do not make mistakes. As we are not enlightened we err. We act out of ignorance. Ignorance is not a person. Ignorance does not need to be attacked. Children often act out of ignorance. What they need at that point is not attack but awareness — knowledge. Ignorance needs not judgment but help. The more we hear the call from within, the more we see that we no longer need judgment.

If anyone is blocking vision and keeping us from enlightenment, it can be only ourselves. It is very helpful to know that no one is to blame. No one else makes us eat compulsively or lie, or creates *lust* within our hearts, or makes us get angry. Nobody!

> *"One's enemies are those of his own house."*
> —Matthew 10:30

The real healing that has to be done in life and the real accomplishments that have to be accomplished must be made within our own house. That is the place to start clearing the path to the Kingdom. Our own house does not mean our husbands, wives, and children. The house is our own being, the place we live inside ourselves as we look out each day upon the world.

To see holiness and hope is to experience richness. It is to live in the Kingdom and know abundance. If we are destructive and hateful, we come from the same fearful place as those who sought to kill Jesus. When we come from love, others cannot help but respond in love. Love does away with the ugly without being malicious. Love melts away fear. Condemnation and projection create fear.

When President Roosevelt used the phrase "the only thing we have to fear is fear itself" in his inaugural address of 1933, the world opened up a little bit in faith and things began to change for the better. People began to believe they could succeed. They began to project faith, trust, and cooperation — instead of fear and anger. Slowly, very slowly, the world began to work again. Actually Roosevelt was wrong.

It is not the case that the only thing we have to fear is fear itself because there is in fact absolutely nothing to be afraid of.

So how shall we deal with anger? The *Course* repeatedly asks us to look at things differently, to choose once again, to realize that there is a better way. It does not ask us to stuff our anger or to pretend we are not angry when in fact we are; that would be denial. It does ask us to realize that if we are angry, a mistake in perception has occurred somewhere and we need another way to look at things.

Exercise No. 6 from the *Workbook* reminds us that if we are upset, we are upset because we see something that is not there.

- We can feel attacked only on an ego level.

- We can experience jealousy only on an ego level.

- We can feel like a failure only on an ego level.

If we really knew who we were, there would be no need to attack or to feel attacked, no need for feelings of betrayal or jealousy.

We need to know that whatever anger we feel cannot be blamed on anyone else. We must assume responsibility for our projections. We do not realize how deep our level of guilt really is. No matter how much peace we may think we feel, we may not realize how much anger is buried inside or how close to the surface it really is.

While I was writing this chapter, I stopped because I noticed that the lid had blown off the trash can out front. Crows had gotten into the can and were strewing paper and garbage all over the driveway. I went out to clean up the mess and put the lid back on the can. The crows flew up into the trees and started screeching at me for disrupting their breakfast. I looked up at one particularly annoying crow and said: "Yeah, well the same to you, too." And I thought to myself, "My goodness, look how close to the surface that was! A crow screeches and you attack back." We need to remember that: *Whatever change needs to happen needs to happen inside me.*

I cannot force change to happen inside someone else. Marianne Williamson, in *Return to Love*, tells how silly her own thinking was when she would get angry because people would not sign her peace petition.

Recognizing that whatever change must take place must take place within me means that if I feel anger coming up I need to stop and see if I cannot look at the situation differently. This requires maturity and an ability to accept responsibility for whatever seems to be happening to us.

Practical Suggestions
for Looking at Our Anger Differently

I want to emphasize that it is not changing our behavior that changes things unless we have first truly changed our minds.

1. Wait a minute

A first step when we notice anger coming up is simply to notice it. Before we start blowing off steam it's helpful just to notice that the steam is coming up.

> *"The best remedy for anger is delay."*
> —Seneca

> *"The best answer to anger is silence."*
> —German Proverb

The old adage about counting to ten is not a bad idea. Counting to sixty is even better — though some people think the reason for delay is to give themselves time to come up with a really good retort. When Julius Caesar was provoked, he used to repeat the entire Roman alphabet before he would speak. From the standpoint of the *Course,* the purpose for delay is simply to give us an opportunity to look at what is happening.

2. Speak softly

There is wisdom also in speaking softly. When confronted with anger remember:

> *"A soft answer turneth away wrath."*
> —Proverbs 15:1

The Speech Research Unit of Kenyon College proved through tests that most people, if shouted at, simply cannot help shouting back. Police hostage rescue teams learn not only what to say but how to speak softly to keep a violent person from becoming more violent.

3. Lighten up

It's helpful to gain a different perspective on a situation through humor and the simple admission and recognition of the part we ourselves are playing in a disruptive situation.

The ego, after all, is really very silly. Anger is always an example of insanity. That is why it is never justified. The *Course* asks us not to take the ego and its world seriously, for this makes it real in our own minds; rather we are urged to laugh gently at the ego and all its seemingly justifiable arrogance.

4. Diffuse the situation

If you can see how silly the situation really is, you might then also be able to diffuse the situation before it gets even crazier.

On her way to investigate a family dispute, San Francisco police officer Adelle Roberts saw a television set crash through the window of the disputants' house. Knocking at the door, Officer Roberts heard the sounds of a heated argument. When a gruff voice demanded "Who is it?" she didn't say, "Police." Instead she said, "TV repairman." Her response dissolved angry shouts into uproarious laughter and set the scene for a peaceful solution.

5. Let it go in a nondestructive way

One day one of the members of our fellowship came in very upset. She said she could not stay for the service, but instead was going to go for a swim. I thought that was a great idea. Going for a swim at a time like that was one of the best things she could do.

One day a friend called to tell me about the weekend she had spent with her daughter and son-in-law. While visiting their home she had experienced an insight into the peculiar quirks of her son-in-law's personality. There was something about him that she felt needed to be fixed. She had written a letter to him and wanted to read it to me before sending it. When she finished reading the letter I said: "Whatever you do, don't send that letter."

She was no doubt right about some of her observations, but I was sure the letter would create a sense of division and would be more hurtful than helpful.

"But," she complained, "I spent two hours on it!"

"Yes," I said, "and, if you feel better, that is all that is necessary."

She threw the letter in the wastebasket and later thanked me, realizing the letter was far too attacking to be helpful.

6. Stop asking – start giving

Anger will never get us what "we think" we want. Though it may get us the other person's attention, it will probably not be the kind of attention we desire. It may bring us compliance, but it does not bring about a change in mind.

Whenever we are angry we are asking the other to change. Just one of the problems in getting the other to change is that in getting what we say we want, we may very well lose.

One semester I was teaching a course on the psychology of religion at Sing Sing prison and as I drove there I would listen to a call-in radio talk show hosted by psychologist Dr. Joy Brown. As I listened, I noticed how often the people who called said they were angry. I also noticed her response. In each instance she tried to show them that if they really succeeded in getting what they said they wanted, they would lose.

If You Win – You Lose

One woman called in "mad as hell" about the way her boyfriend showered gifts on his adult daughter. She said she wanted him to stop it and wanted the girl to stop being so selfish. Dr. Brown suggested that if she got what she said she wanted, she would no doubt create a sense of separation between herself, her boyfriend, and his daughter — and she might very well lose her boyfriend in the process. In essence, though not quoting the *Course,* she said:

*"Let him be what he is
and seek not to make of love an enemy."*
—T.394; T-19.IV.D.i.13:8

When we are angry we are asking for something. When we feel anger coming up, it is helpful to stop for a moment. What are you asking for? Could you perhaps let it go? Instead of asking, give something. Let the truth prevail. Recognize your own responsibility in the situation. It will be much more healing.

If you would know God, says Jesus, turn within. If there is any purification that needs to be done, do that purification within. There is nothing out there that needs to be destroyed. Evil is in the eye of the beholder, as is love. Look upon the world with condemnation and we experience condemnation. Look upon the world with love and others respond to us in love.

The Poverty of Self-Righteousness

Jesus teaches trust and ever-increasing faith in God. He teaches trust even to the point of seeming betrayal. The destruction of the body by those who live in fear is nothing, for they cannot kill the soul. Hitler lived in and taught fear. He projected onto the Jews responsibility for whatever evil existed in the world and used that projection to justify his insane attack on them. Those who killed Jesus lived in fear. But Christ lives in absolute love. Christ cannot be destroyed. You cannot be destroyed. Jesus went to the cross to show us there isn't anything to be afraid of.

In *Star Wars* Obewan Kenobe and Darth Vader duel with their laser swords. As they are fighting Obewan Kenobe says to Darth Vader, "Strike me down and I'll become a thousand times more powerful." At the right moment he is struck down, and we are assured that his energy has been released for greater good. The same thing happened with Jesus. Those who would attack and kill one who stands for love end up demonstrating that the spirit of love cannot be destroyed. Strangely, they get just the opposite effect from what they want. You cannot kill a Jesus, a Martin Luther King, Jr., or a Gandhi.

In the crucifixion of Jesus, a message and a ministry confined to a tiny piece of geography was made available to all the world. The Pharisees struck out in ignorance, anger, and misperception. Jesus went to the cross to show us that attack never works.

The self-righteous are always in danger of betrayal by the ego. Those most self-righteous are least likely to be right-minded. They are most likely to engage in the insanity of attacking other children of God in the name of God. The Pharisees of Jesus' day were religious people with such large beams in their eyes they could not see their own projections.

> *"I tell you solemnly,*
> *tax collectors and prostitutes*
> *are making their way*
> *into the Kingdom of God before you."*
> —Matthew 21:31

The meticulous lawkeepers, who had forgotten the spirit of the law for the sake of its letter, were themselves the most incapable of recognizing darkness within. The tax collectors and prostitutes at least knew they were uncentered and in need of better perception. The Pharisees could not see that they were in their own way. They could not see darkness lurking within and so attempted to find dirt in a man who was clean. Religious fanatics, extreme rightists and leftists run the same risk today. Their rightness is always in terms of others being wrong.

When anger comes up, forgiveness and joining are needed. When Jesus in the *Course* says that our brother is part of us, he means it literally. This other person you are about to become furious with — is you.

Jesus makes it clear that what is needed is forgiveness, and forgiveness recognizes that what you thought your brother did to you never happened. Forgiveness does not pardon sin and make it real. Forgiveness sees there was no sin. It recognizes that the peace and love of God are still within you, regardless of any mistakes your brother or you may have made.

*"Forgiveness, on the other hand,
is still and quietly does nothing.
It offends no aspect of reality,
nor seeks to twist it to appearances it likes.
It merely looks, and waits, and judges not."*
—W.391; W-401.4:1-3

Chapter 11

Making Something of Nothing: The Defense of the Atonement

The *Course* also talks about the Atonement as a defense. However, while ego defenses can be used destructively, *the Atonement cannot be use destructively. It cannot be turned into a weapon of attack.* All other defenses are inherently defenses of attack. The defense of the Atonement *cannot be misused* but *it can be refused.* It cannot hurt. It can only heal.

According to traditional Christian theology, the Atonement is the effect of Jesus' suffering and death in redeeming humankind. I have a book of illustrations for use by Christian ministers. Each of the twelve illustrations it offers regarding the Atonement describes the suffering, bleeding, dying sacrifice that Jesus made for our sins. Yet to talk about Christ dying for our sins reinforces rather than releases our sense of guilt. If he died for my sin, then I must be guilty of that sin. I must have been responsible for his death. This is a heavy load of guilt for anyone to bear.

According to *The Encyclopedia of Religion*, the theme of all Christian doctrines of the Atonement can be expressed in the sentence, "Christ died for our sins."

In Judaism, Yom Kippur, the Day of Atonement, the most solemn holiday of the Jewish year, is to be a day of fasting and repenting of sins. The way the Atonement process has been traditionally understood makes sin real. Then we must try to forgive the sin or seek to have it forgiven.

As a Christian minister, I always had trouble with this doctrine and could never preach it. It was not until I found the *Course* that I understood the Atonement. The *Course* says that if we focus on suffering, bleeding, and dying we make the body real — and the *Course* is very clear that we are not bodies. According to the *Course: The Atonement is never completed by fighting.*

The Atonement is not accomplished by fighting against sin. The purpose of the Atonement is to dispel illusions, not to establish them as real and then try to vanquish them. The hymn "Onward, Christian Soldiers, Marching as to War" is a contradiction in terms. War is totally contradictory to the teaching of Jesus. We cannot root out evil as though it were some horrible weed. Evil is overcome as we come to understand our reality as children of God. There is nothing destructive about the truth, which is why the defense of the Atonement cannot be used destructively.

The Atonement is not accomplished by beating one's breast and saying "Mea Culpa, Mea Culpa" ("I am guilty"). It comes as we recognize that the little, seemingly guilty self I thought myself to be has nothing to do with who I really am. We are all children of God; we cannot help being such. When we see who we really are, we cannot even think in terms of separation or of harming anyone or anything. On the level of the ego there is, of course, much separation, many misperceptions or errors that need to be corrected. But we do not correct error by waging war. War compounds error.

Reparation or Awakening

According to traditional Christianity what is needed is reparation for sin to atone for waywardness. According to the *Course* what is needed is an awakening — a coming to a realization of the Self we already are, not a furtherance of illusion. What is needed is an awareness of our inherent innocence, not our inherent guilt. The *Course* says that innocence is wisdom because it is unaware of evil (T.33; T-3.II.2).

Jesus never fought against sin. He took no time to defend himself before Pilate. He went to the cross recognizing that his crucifiers were caught in an illusion. Jesus from the cross says:

"Father, forgive them
for they know not what they are doing."

He said this, not because God had to be instructed on how to handle the situation, but so we would learn that no matter how persecuted we might seem to be, our only task is one of forgiveness. Our need is to see things differently, to overcome the belief in separation. This is the process of the Atonement. "The Atonement is the Holy Spirit's plan of correction, for undoing the ego, thus healing our belief in separation. The Atonement came into being with the creation of the Holy Spirit after the separation, and will be completed when every separated son of God has fulfilled his part in the Atonement through total forgiveness" (Ken Wapnick, *Glossary Index for A Course in Miracles*, p. 27).

Overcoming Separation

The ego thinks of itself as being separate from (other than) God. Insofar as we experience our lives as lost, painful, and ego-bound, we know nothing of the Kingdom of Heaven. According to the *Course,* after the separation occurred the Atonement became necessary so we could get back to God (T.16; T-20).

We may think of the separation in symbolic terms as representative of what happened with Adam and Eve in the Garden. The separation is also something that happens in each of us as we think of ourselves as being separated from — other than — a part of God's family. Before the Fall, there was no need for the Atonement, as there was no separation. Everything was complete. There was only wholeness. After the separation it was necessary to set up conditions to overcome the separation.

"The Atonement principle was in effect
long before the Atonement began.
The principle was love
and the Atonement was an act of love.
Acts were not necessary before the separation,
because belief in space and time did not exist.

*It was only after the separation that the Atonement
and the conditions necessary for its fulfillment were planned."*
                    –T.16; T-2.II.4:2-5

As we grow from infancy through childhood the ego progressively dominates our life. The ego's hold on our identity grows with every painful experience that seems to teach us that we are alone, apart and separate.

- As an infant I bang my toe in the end of the crib. It is painful. This experience tells me that I am a body and that it is possible to be hurt.

- Mother walks out of the room as I lie crying in my crib, and I again experience separation.

- I go to school and am teased by my peers because of the way I am dressed — and more separation occurs.

As each of these experiences befalls us the ego develops and is reinforced. We go into ourselves and get caught up in complicated, unforgiving, knots of resistance and anger. This continues each time I experience myself being beaten by sticks and stones and words that really do seem to hurt.

Complexes, Coexes, and Hang-ups

Psychologists talk about complexes or what Dr. Stanislof Grof calls coexes, or blocks in the psychic system. These complexes form around each place in which I feel rejected, hurt, or separated. Eventually there is a whole complex of knots, all tangled and wound around as in a great ball of string. The greater the complexity of these knots the more difficult it is for me to see or understand clearly. Using the Atonement as a defense means undoing these knots. It is, as the *Course* expresses it, a

*"removal of the blocks
to an awareness of love's presence."*

Imagine that you have some great ball of string bound in a series of knots. If you have ever tried to untangle such a mess, you know it may be complicated and frustrating. We can think of each of these knots as a place in the psychic system where we are hung up or attached. The more we try to defend these knots, the tighter they become. If you tell a lie to defend another lie you now have two lies. The tighter we pull the knots together, the more we turn these complexes into full-blown soap operas — often with dramatic effects. The more complicated the mess and the greater the strength of the ego defense, the more impossible it seems to be to able to unravel the whole thing.

Clearing Out the Knots

Almost everyone has had the experience of trying to undo the knots in a ball of string, a gold chain, a garden hose, or an electrical cord. As you begin to clear up some of the knots, other knots somehow also miraculously clear up along the way. Loosening things up in one area suddenly brings a whole length of new chain, or wire, or hose, or string. In the same way, as the Atonement begins to work within us we experience new freedom in our psychic system.

Let's say I discover that I don't need to drink any more, or do drugs. Stopping the drinking and the drugs may clear up lots of other problems.

- I may discover that I have more self-assurance, poise, confidence, and energy for my work.

- I may start getting along better with my colleagues.

- I may suddenly be wasting less time and earning more money. Clearing up what seemed to be one problem has consequences across the spectrum.

This is what the *Course* means by a miracle — a release — an undoing of some mess in my mind that kept me from seeing. Just as the defense of the ego creates bigger messes, the defense of the Atonement undoes messes. The Atonement process is the means by which we can let go of the places we are hung up till we are totally free — thereby returning to innocence and the knowledge of our existence in the Kingdom of God.

The Atonement calls upon us to reevaluate everything. As we let go of the chaff — as we give up illusions — the truth of who we already are must come to the fore.

The Atonement enables us to escape from everything that we thought we were and thus facilitates the process of awakening. Accepting the Atonement means realizing that all the ego stuff we thought was real meant nothing. Having built a complicated case for a messy psychic system, I now realize that the whole thing doesn't matter, that it doesn't make any sense, that it's insane and therefore meaningless. It's all part of an illusory world or a dream. It exists only in space and time, which is part of the illusion.

In the process of unwinding these knots or complexes we begin to see that there isn't anything there in the first place. My ego may have gotten hung up or caught on something, but what it got caught on is meaningless. I may have made something out of being rejected as a child, a wound that became swollen and sore. In order to heal I need to forgive or let go of the past. Indeed, the Atonement is the process by which we free ourselves from the past (T.17; T-2.II.6). It is often easy to see this in a friend. We can see that the place in which he seems to be hung up or something over which she is worrying is really silly. It is of course more difficult to see such hang-ups in ourselves.

As with all problems, ultimately it doesn't make any sense. It's nothing. Once a problem is in the past, we often wonder why it was a problem. We've probably all had the experience of being hung up on a relationship that we eventually got over and then looked back and could not imagine why we were so hung up over that particular person.

> *"The Atonement is the device*
> *by which you can free yourself*
> *from the past as you go ahead.*
> *It undoes your past errors,*
> *thus making it unnecessary*
> *for you to keep retracing your steps..."*
> −T.17; T-2.II.6:4-5

There Is Nothing There

When you work the knots out of a chain and get to the end (or the beginning), you discover that there was nothing there. There was nothing that caused the knot in the first place. Or it was just some "kinky" little thing that really was nothing. To put it another way, the ego causes the knots in our psyches and the ego is nothing. When we begin to undo the messes we have made for ourselves and we get the whole thing straightened out there is nothing there. There never was anything there; we just thought there was. That's illusion.

One Self

To come to an awareness of love's presence means to let go of all the places inside the psyche where I have been hung up, attached, hurt. As I do this I come to an awareness of God's very active presence in my life, not as something other, but as an inner Identity much more real than the sniffling little ego I once thought I was.

The ego seeks to build its own world, but it is ultimately doomed to failure. The other alternative is to align oneself with God. Everyone is our brother and our sister. We are all quite literally one with God whether we see it or not. When we see that we are one with everyone, we are at one with God. For this reason, whenever we give anything of ourselves, we are giving it to ourselves — because there is no difference between us. We are quite literally One Self united with our creator. In seeing and accepting this One Self our Atonement is complete.

In the Atonement we see that the other is us. When we first fall in love, we discover another self that is us. It is easy for us to give to people we love because we don't see difference between us. It is thus that I may think of my lover, my wife, my husband, my child as myself.

Accepting the Atonement means not giving in to fearful dreams of sickness and death. It is the recognition that God has created us perfect, and that is the only way we can be.

- To accept the Atonement means not to be alone. It is the end of separation.

- To accept the Atonement means the experience of perfect love.

- Acceptance of the Atonement is just a matter of time.

It's what Jesus did. It is what any of us could do.

No matter how far any of us may have wandered, no matter how complicated the knot, no matter how great the gulf that seems to separate us, it can all be undone in an instant. It is as simple as waking up. It is a matter of a realization. When we realize something, we make real what is real and relinquish the false.

Jesus made no distinction in loving. He loved everyone, saint and sinner. When the Atonement is complete in us we love everyone — saint and sinner.

Atonement Means Commitment

The Atonement involves total commitment to the truth. That's all, just total commitment to the truth, to love, and to the fulfillment of who we are. It is the treasure hidden in the field, the pearl of great price, one's all and everything. It is the experience of the true condition of the Son of God. It is the ultimate experience of God.

The experience of the Kingdom of Heaven is the only really meaningful and worthwhile experience. There is no greater joy, no higher fulfillment than being at home. The Atonement is the recognition that the separation never occurred. It was only a dream. We cannot, in fact, be separate from God (T.90; T-6.II).

Whenever we are afraid, in pain, or lonely, we need to remember that we are already one with God. When we look upon others as ourselves and give freely, we see that the Atonement is already complete. Use the Atonement as your defense. It is the only one that will work. If we hurt our brother — we hurt ourselves. Jesus on the cross is invulnerable. Invulnerability is really the only way things can be.

The Self that we really are has already completed the Atonement. As egos we never will. At any moment any one of us could awaken from our fearful dreaming of the world and see ourselves once again as children of God.

Completing the Atonement is why we are here. It is the natural profession of the children of God (T.6; T-1.III.10). To complete the Atonement is to know that you can never die.

> *"My part in the Atonement is the canceling out of all errors*
> *that you could not otherwise correct.*
> *When you have been restored to the recognition*
> *of your original state,*
> *you naturally become part of the Atonement yourself.*
> *As you share my unwillingness to accept error*
> *in yourself and others,*
> *you must join the great crusade to correct it;*
> *listen to my voice,*
> *learn to undo error and act to correct it.*
> *The power to work miracles belongs to you.*
> *I will provide the opportunity to do them,*
> *but you must be ready and willing.*
> *Doing them will bring conviction in the ability,*
> *because conviction comes through accomplishment.*
> *The ability is the potential,*
> *the achievement is its expression,*
> *and the Atonement,*
> *which is the natural profession of the children of God,*
> *is the purpose."*
> —T.6; T-1.III.1:4-10

Part II

Application of the Course

Chapter 12

From Specialness to Holiness

"The Holy Spirit knows no one is special."
—T.291; T-15.V.5:1

*"As travelers meet by chance along the way,
so does a man meet wife, children, relatives and friends:
let him therefore be in the world and yet separate from it."*
—Srimad Bhagavavatam

One of the most obvious facts of life is that there are other people in this world. Not only is no man an island — no one would want to be. The presence of others gives us our greatest joy as well as our deepest concerns. The *Course* says we enter into the Kingdom of Heaven only by joining, and Heaven is found only through a *"collaborative venture."* We enter Heaven holding on one side the hand of someone who has helped us and on the other the hand of someone we have helped. We are at every moment each other's teachers.

"Every relationship becomes a lesson in love."
—T.291; T-15.V.4:6

As ego-oriented beings, we all develop what the *Course* refers to as special relationships. In everyday parlance, the word, "special" generally has a positive connotation, meaning one thing as opposed to another. Within the *Course*, special relationship means "specialness." It means finding some "special" person with some "special gifts" who makes me feel "special."

Enter Guilt

Guilt according to the *Course* is what keeps the ego intact. It is "ego glue" or "ego mortar."

> *"The ego establishes relationships only to get something.*
> *And it would keep the giver bound to itself through guilt....*
> *For it is the ego's fundamental doctrine*
> *that what you do to others you have escaped.*
> *The ego wishes no one well."*
> —T.295; T-15.VII.2:1-2; 4:2-3

Special relationships are ones in which we are attached, hung up, dependent, angry, neurotic. They are relationships in which we have things to work out in order to attain peace. In this sense all our relationships are special because we want to "look good" in other people's eyes.

> *"Everyone on earth has formed special relationships,*
> *and although this is not so in Heaven,*
> *the Holy Spirit knows how*
> *to bring a touch of Heaven to them here."*
> —T.291; T-15.V.8:1

We can and do develop special relationships with people, animals, food, money, clothing, cigarettes, alcohol and drugs, our homes, our cars, our work, and institutions such as the church or the government. A special relationship is based on the belief that we are in some way lacking and that one of these special things has what we need to make us complete. We may thus believe that if we just had the "right" kind of relationship or the "right" job or a certain amount of money everything would be okay.

We develop special relationships with our mothers and fathers, husbands, wives, sisters, brothers, teachers, landlords, tenants, employers, employees, etc. We use these special relationships to build defenses against the truth of our reality as spiritual beings.

All relationships *in this world* begin with the perception of separation. Indeed, the infant becomes progressively aware of *self* as it also becomes progressively aware of "mother" as someone "other than" me.

The first special relationship described in the Bible is that of Adam and Eve as they perceived themselves as separate from or other than God. Special relationships inevitably exclude God, though it is God we are seeking in our relationships.

According to the *Course* we develop special relationships in two distinct ways — either as special hate or special love. Special hate justifies the projection of guilt by attack (T.294-97; T-316-20). Special love conceals attack within the illusion of love.

> *"The special love relationship*
> *is the ego's chief weapon*
> *for keeping you from Heaven."*
> —T.317; T-16.V.2:3

Special Hate

Special hate is actually easier to understand than special love because the lines of separation are more clearly drawn. There is more black and white in the relationship — less gray. Examples of special hate have been America's relationship with the Russians, the relationship between blacks and whites, teenagers and adults, leftists and rightists, fundamentalists and newagers, pro-life and pro-choice.

When we hate, it is clear to us that we are absolutely right and the other is absolutely wrong. It is thus clear that the other deserves our animosity and condemnation. In each special hate relationship we get to luxuriate in the feeling that our anger is justifiable and/or excusable as the other is so obviously wrong.

It is sometimes easier to work through special hate than special love relationships because the division is clearly defined and the need to work through the relationship is great. We see this in the work going on between the United States and Russia to find a solution to past differences. Special love relationships are sometimes more difficult to work through because the dynamics of guilt and projection are *masked* in the relationship. After all, *it is a love relationship,* so we don't want to think of it as unpleasant or see it as based on guilt.

Special Love:
Our Parents / Our Children / Ourselves

Our first special relationships are, of course, with our parents. As we get older we develop similar special relationships with members of our peer group, our teachers, our employers and/or employees, with our colleagues, friends, and in turn with our children. Our special relationships are primarily developed with our major companions in life: parents, mates, and children — though you might have a special relationship, which lasts only a minute, as you yell out your car window, seeking to reinforce guilt in the driver who just cut you off.

"He that loves father or mother more than me is not worthy of me;
and he that loves son or daughter more than me is not worthy of me".
−Matthew 11:37

As we get hung up in our relationships with our parents and children and they in turn get hung up in their relationships with us, we miss the Kingdom of Heaven.

"The first half of our lives is ruined by our parents
and the second by our children."
−Clarence Darrow

I had a friend who had a bumper sticker on her car that read:

"Avenge yourself,
live long enough to become a problem to your children."

The relationship we have with our parents is the most basic, as it begins at birth and extends until death. Even if we are not in direct contact with our parents we have a psychological relationship with them. Freud was no doubt right about the significance of our feelings toward our mothers and fathers, and the need we all have to be at peace with them and resolve our feelings of guilt in relation to them.

The *Course* says that all relationships are teaching assignments. Though it may remain a mystery to us, we no doubt each have the parents we do in order to learn what the Holy Spirit would teach us.

As children we are dependent upon our parents and our self-image takes form within the framework of that relationship.

- If we are rejected, we develop feelings of unworthiness and self-blame.

- If we are loved and accepted, we develop feelings of self-worth.

Regardless of our learning, each of us develops special feelings that need resolution.

> *"Psychiatry enables us to correct our faults*
> *by confessing our parents' shortcomings."*
> —Joey Adams

As a part of my graduate training in counseling, I was required to spend some time in psychoanalysis. My therapist wanted to focus on talking about my parents. My parents were not perfect, but I could not understand why it was necessary to focus so much attention on problems with people who had contributed so much to my life. As a young man I was much more concerned with getting on with my future than rehashing my past. My father was already beginning to show signs of the early onset of Alzheimer's. Why should I project onto him responsibility for problems I might have?

Growing up on a farm my father and I worked a great deal together and thus developed a bond that occurs when you spend many hours laboring together. I am grateful for many clear memories of gassing up the tractor as the sun was coming up on the horizon, cleaning tools in the garage, his whimsical smile and his distinctive cough.

He loved to help me with my math. He taught me how to fix cars and manage money. We never talked about women or sex or philosophy or religion. These were things I needed to learn from other guides. But he did what he could, what he knew how to do. He cannot be faulted for not having known more. None of our parents should be blamed for their imperfections any more than any of us wish to be blamed for our imperfections.

Holding On Perpetuates Pain

The Bible tells us that the sins of the parents are visited on the children unto the second and third generation. But blaming our parents, spouse, or children for our shortcomings is a poor parody of life. At some point the sin has to stop. We can stop it by relinquishing whatever we were holding on to as hurting in our relationship and becoming responsible for our own healing.

Many years ago I heard Dr. Elisabeth Kübler-Ross estimate that 25 percent of all children are abused. That figure is now thought to be conservative. If we take into account psychological and emotional abuse, the real figure is certainly higher. Healing that kind of experience may seem a formidable task. But continuing to hold on and projecting guilt only perpetuates the pain. Keeping the experience alive makes it likely that abusive patterns will recur in our relationships as adults.

As adults we need to forgive our parents (living or dead) so we can get on with other relationships. In talking with my mother on the phone one day, I realized how little time we actually have with each other, how little time we may yet have together, and I thought what a silly waste of time it is to share anything but love.

We need to forgive our parents for not having been other than who they were — for not having been more intelligent, richer or more loving. We need to drop the blame and accept the reality that our parents are (were) who they are (were).

> *"Forgiveness is giving up all hope of having a better past."*
> —Gerald Jampolsky

The good news is that we are free to choose love now. As parents ourselves, we need to accept our children for being who they are and get on with loving them.

Geraldo Rivera's TV show once featured "heavyset girls and their mothers." One girl said that she wished her mother would just leave her alone about her weight. She said she was happily married, her husband did not bother her, and she wished her mother would get off her back. The microphone then went to the mother who said: "Well if I don't ride her about this, who will?" Truth is, if there is anybody riding any of us about any problem we have, there is nobody riding us more than we ride ourselves. We know what we need to do — nobody else has to tell us. If you have a problem like being overweight, there is no one more aware of that problem than you are.

"Let your children go if you want to keep them."
—Malcolm Forbes

No one likes to be the recipient of criticism, and criticism is even harder to take when it comes from our mothers or fathers or husbands or wives. If your financial advisor tells you that you are wasting your money, it is one thing. If your mother tells you you are wasting your money, she is the last person you want to hear it from.

We are ourselves responsible for being here. To be happy we need to let go of all grievances about the past. Only the decision I am making right now — and not anything that happened in the past — can keep me from the experience of love. Only our own decision to heal and to forgive can fill our lives with the Love that is always ours.

The Only Real Love

"Love of God is the one essential thing."
—Swami Ramakrishna

Ultimately the *Course* asks us to drop all of our special relationships because we have no need for them.

*"Hear him gladly, and learn of Him
that you have no need of special relationships at all."*
—T.298; T-15.V.III.2:1

There is only one relationship that will ever be completely satisfying. There is only one purpose for our being in this world, and that is to fulfill or complete that relationship. We have but one task and that is to remember God.

As the medieval mystic Meister Eckhart expressed it:

*"Become in all things a God seeker
and in all things a God finder
at all times and in all places."*

After all, what we are seeking in our special relationships is God. While no one else can be God for us, we may come to know God as we share our love in relationships.

The *Course* not only talks about special relationships; it also talks about holy relationships. It's easy to misinterpret what a holy relationship is. Diane says that when she first heard of a holy relationship in the *Course*, she thought it was a very special special relationship. In the holy relationship we begin to look at things the way they really are rather than the way we have fantasized them to be. A holy relationship is the Holy Spirit's means to undo guilt by shifting the goal of the relationship to forgiveness and truth.

Holy relationships are not a matter of flowers and pretty songs. Holy relationships confront us with the reality of who we really are, and the ego, as we have seen, likes to hide out so it does not have to look at reality. Just as special relationships are relationships in which we hide from the Self, so holy relationships give us the opportunity to meet our Self and thus begin to awaken to our own call.

> *"Every special relationship you have made has,*
> *as its fundamental purpose,*
> *the aim of occupying your mind so completely*
> *that you will not hear the call of truth."*
> —T.333; T-17.IV.3:3

As we come to have a fulfilling relationship with God so do we come to fulfilling relationships with our Self and with others. Relationships work insofar as we have a positive working relationship with God.

Love and Marriage

Several studies have been made of people who claim to have happy marriages. What makes for the best marriages makes for the best friendships, the best sibling relationships, the best employer/employee relationships, etc. We are not talking about perfect relationships; we're talking about good "working" relationships in which we are moving together in love seeking peace and releasing pain.

Those who have the best marriages tend to view their partner as their best friend and like the other person as a human being. If we were wise enough during the initial period of falling in love we might look at this other person and ask:

- "Is this someone I would like to be with if I were not in love?"

- "Is this someone I feel I can work things out with?"

- "Is there openness here to the experience and expression of forgiveness?"

Forget about romantic love and cathecting. Do you like your partner? Do you respect this other person for being who that person is? If you were not married to this person would you like to have him or her as a friend?

Why does the wife like the husband? Largely because the husband likes and respects the wife. It's all reminiscent of Jesus' saying that we should *do unto others as we would have others do unto us.* Happy couples are willing to give more than they receive. While aware of the flaws in their mates, they are also aware of the likable qualities, which are seen as more important than the deficiencies.

In this way, each of us, as we chooses a life's mate, really choose a companion with whom we will be working things through, seeking together the entrance to the Kingdom. Staying together in this sense means not running away at the first sign of trouble. Commitment is thus the willingness to "work things out," to go though periods of being unhappy with the thought that things will get better. As one lady married for many years expressed it: "Love is what you've been through with somebody."

When older people marry, they do so for companionship. Sex is not a major concern. Romantic love isn't a big reason. Companionship is the reason. A *companion* is quite literally someone who "accompanies" us in the life journey. A company or fellowship is a group of people who come together to work and play together. We have companions because we want to share our life.

We founded Interfaith Fellowship with the thought that it could be a place where people could grow, work, play, pray, cry, and laugh together. It is a place where we can be open to the discovery of true forgiveness. True forgiveness is the recognition that there is nothing to forgive. Once there is nothing to forgive, all you have is love.

In order to experience Heaven in a relationship the negative aspects of the special relationship must fall away. There is no room in Heaven for dependencies, attachments, hang-ups, anger, or hatred. There is no place for envy, apprehension, or bitterness. Heaven, by definition, is a place of freedom and truth, a purified state in which ego problems are worked through. Nothing is lost but everything is gained. We can then be at one with God and our companions.

Jesus says there is no marriage in Heaven. To say there is no marriage in Heaven means there are no special relationships in Heaven. No one can be the property of another. To invest in another as our primary reality is to miss the greater love of God.

A growing segment of our society is making the choice to remain single. Marriage is not always necessary and the happier we are with ourselves and our relationships with others, the less need we may have to be married. After all, married or not, our primary relationship is the one we have with God.

Only by recognizing what is really valuable can we begin to gain what is really valuable. Ultimately all relationships are for the undoing of guilt. They are here for us to practice forgiveness — for letting things be, for finding the way back to Heaven.

The *Course* would ask us not to make anyone special. Don't put anyone on a pedestal. Don't put anyone down. None of us has any idea how far another is along the way. Our task is to accept others as they are, as we would have ourselves accepted. We are all entitled to our own choices and mistakes. We are not here to "correct" each other. We are here to love each other.

Eternity in the Other

Perfect love casts out fear, and perfect love is possible. This is not attached, conditional love; it's not even a feeling, but real love. As God loves us, so can we love each other. The freshness of love need not be lost, and we can go on giving without concern for past or future.

It is always possible to drop fears, both of things that have happened to us and of things that might happen in the future.

It is always possible to move into the eternal now, where love can be experienced purely. The truth is, there is more eternity in the other than any of us will ever know while we live within the confines of the ego.

Forgiving the illusions we hold of others and ourselves, reaching past all idolatry to truth, it is possible to enter into relationships in which we work together toward the Kingdom of God. The *Course* says that no one who loves can judge. In the holy relationship we learn to drop all judgment.

- There is no need for possessiveness or jealously.

- There is no need for blame or hurt or pain.

- There is no need to be looking for someone to fulfill us.

The only completely fulfilling relationship is that which we have with God.

> *"No life can express,*
> *nor tongue so much as name*
> *what this enflaming, all-conquering love of God is.*
> *It is brighter than the sun;*
> *it is sweeter that anything that is called sweet;*
> *it is stronger than all strength;*
> *it is more nutrimental than food;*
> *more cheering to the heart than wine,*
> *and more pleasant than all the joy*
> *and pleasantness of this world.*
> *Whosoever obtaineth it,*
> *is richer than any monarch born on earth;*
> *and he who getteth it,*
> *is more noble than any emperor can be,*
> *and more potent and absolute*
> *than all power and authority."*
>
> —Medieval mystic Jacob Boehm

There is no thing in this world that can ultimately satisfy us. No one is here to fulfill us. That does not mean we are not to joyfully celebrate our loving relationships. If, however, we think that by sustaining the form of one particular relationship we will attain salvation, we misperceive the reality that can be alive only inside of us. As a friend once said: "We are not seeking our soulmate; we are seeking our soul."

The message of the *Course* is that we are already complete, and the only way we can be really happy is to love everyone the way God loves us, without discrimination, without specialness, without expectation, without demand. God is our only goal, our only love; we have no love but Him. As God becomes the object of our love, when we have no goal but Him, all other loves shall be ours as well — not detached and dependent love, but love that is free and flowing and open to forgiveness.

All the love in the universe is ours when our primary relationship is with God. The *Course* asks us to relate only to that which will never leave us and what we can ourselves never leave (T.298; T-15.VIII.3:1). All the parts are joined in God through Christ, when they become like to the Father.

> *"Your relationships are with the universe.*
> *And this universe, being of God,*
> *is far beyond the petty sum*
> *of all the separate bodies you perceive.*
> *For all its parts are joined in God though Christ,*
> *where they become like to their Father."*
> —T.299; T-15.VIII.4:4-6

To find ourselves in God is to be Self-fulfilling.

> *"Love wishes to be known,*
> *completely understood and shared.*
> *It has no secrets;*
> *nothing that it would keep apart and hide.*
> *It walks in sunlight, open-eyed and calm,*
> *in smiling welcome and in sincerity*
> *so simple and so obvious it cannot be misunderstood."*
> —T.406; T-20.VI.2:5-7

Chapter 13

There Is Nothing to Forgive

The following is a dialogue between a husband and a wife:

HUSBAND: "Why do you keep talking about my past mistakes? I thought you had forgiven and forgotten."

WIFE: "I have, indeed, forgiven and forgotten. But I don't want you to forget that I have forgiven and forgotten."

If there is any idea that is central to *A Course in Miracles* it is forgiveness. The Foundation for *A Course in Miracles* chose as its logo a stylized design of the word "forgiveness." Dr. Kenneth Wapnick's first major work after his glossary and other introductory material was *Forgiveness and Jesus*. Obviously he wants us to understand the nature of forgiveness and the incredible power it has to change our lives.

False Forgiveness

According to the *Course* the ego has its own version of forgiveness, which is not true forgiveness. In fact, it is not forgiveness at all, but masquerades as forgiveness.

> *"The ego's plan is to have you see error clearly first,*
> *then overlook it.*
> *Yet how can you overlook what you have made real?*
> *By seeing it clearly,*
> *you have made it real and cannot overlook it."*
> —T.157; T-9.IV.4:4-6

First the ego must see the existence of sin; then it places itself literally in a "holier-than-thou" position from which others may be "forgiven" for the wrong they have done. This is the usual position we take in forgiving another, but this is not forgiveness. To understand forgiveness we need a complete reversal in the way we see things; we need a perspective outside the realm of the ego.

A Sunday School teacher asked one of the boys in her class what we must do before we can expect to be forgiven of sin. She was, of course, expecting the boy to say we must first repent. But he carried it back one step further and said: "First we must sin." This is the way it is in traditional Christianity. First we provide testimony to the reality of sin, and then we try to overlook it. But the confirmation of the reality of sin makes forgiveness impossible, as we cannot forgive a sin we believe is real. Someone once said, "No one forgets where the hatchet is buried."

In the realm of the ego it is indeed true that no one forgets where the hatchet is buried. We may pretend that we have forgiven, but how can we possibly forgive a sin we believe is real?

> *"Unjustified forgiveness is attack.*
> *And this is all the world can ever give.*
> *It pardons 'sinners' sometimes,*
> *but remains aware that they have sinned.*
> *And so they do not merit the forgiveness that it gives.*
> *This is the false forgiveness*
> *which the world employs to keep the sense of sin alive."*
> —T.594; T-30.VI.3:5-8, 4:1

Jesus looks past the outer appearance to the reality of the Self. In the story of the Anointing at Bethany, as in many other instances, the disciples are amazed that Jesus does not see the woman in question as they do — namely, someone with an unsavory reputation. The truth is that Jesus recognizes who she *really is*, not a sinner but, like himself, a child of God. In the same way he asks us to look past seeming differences that reflect separation.

We help others to have the experience of forgiveness by helping them awaken to their own true identity, not by continuing to pour upon them the illusion of guilt and sin. We cannot confirm another's true reality by offering testimony to a sinful, sick, and saddened life, but only by recognizing the other for who they really are — true children of God.

Forgiveness as a Reciprocal Process

Just as giving is a preface to receiving and judging is a preface to being judged, so forgiveness prefaces our experience of being forgiven. There are thirteen times that Jesus talks about forgiveness in the Gospels. In each of those instances — as, for example, in the Lord's Prayer — he always teaches that:

"As you forgive, so are you forgiven."

"If you can see your brother merits pardon,
you have learned forgiveness is your right as much as his."
—T.594; T-30.VI.4:7

This is strong teaching; it makes it clear that the responsibility of forgiving and being forgiven is ours, and we truly do not understand forgiveness or what it means to be the recipient of forgiveness until we first forgive.

Just before Leonardo da Vinci commenced work on his "Last Supper," he had a violent quarrel with a fellow painter. So enraged and bitter was Leonardo that he determined to paint the face of his enemy, the other artist, into the face of Judas; thus would he take his revenge, handing the man down in infamy and scorn to succeeding generations. The face of Judas was the first that he finished, and everyone could easily recognize it as the face of the painter with whom he had quarreled.

When Leonardo came to paint the face of Christ, he could make no progress. Something seemed to be thwarting him, holding him back, frustrating his best efforts. Eventually, he painted out the face of Judas and commenced anew on the face of Jesus, this time with success. We cannot at the same time try to paint the features of Christ into our own life and paint a brother's face with the colors of enmity and hatred. Thus it is that, as we learn to forgive, so do we experience ourselves what forgiveness is.

The more frightened we are and the more we are caught in our ego structure, the more sin, sickness, and sadness look very real. A fearful mind seeks to make illusions real.

- As we make our fears real we ignore the peace of God.

- As we make hell real;

- as we value that which is valueless;

- as we find the world and the people in it sick, sad, and despairing;

- as we fear the future, we promote the idea of hell.

As we promote the idea of hell, we cannot see peace. We cannot see God. God does not judge us but loves us under all conditions. The statement, "May God forgive you your sins," is a strange parody, for our loving Father does not bring condemnation upon us.

> *"The grace of God rests gently on forgiving eyes,*
> *and everything they look on speaks of Him to the beholder.*
> *He can see no evil; nothing in the world to fear,*
> *and no one who is different from himself."*
> —T.492; T-25.VI.1, 2

By projecting onto others the need for God's forgiveness, we try to make sin real in them and ourselves. To make sin real and then try to forgive it affirms its reality. Our pardon then becomes a vain attempt to overlook what we think is true. If we make an illusion real, the pardon we offer to the world is a deception. We don't really forgive, and we show that we do not by hanging on to our accusations of sin.

> *"The major difficulty that you find*
> *in genuine forgiveness on your part*
> *is that you still believe you must forgive the truth*
> *and not illusions.*
> *For it is impossible to think of sin as true*
> *and not believe forgiveness is a lie."*
> —W.242; W-134.3:1, 4:2

To witness sin and then try to forgive it is backward thinking. Concentration on error is only further error. We demonstrate our knowledge of Heaven by showing others that their so-called sins have no effect. We can demonstrate, as Jesus did, that we cannot be betrayed.

> *"It is not difficult to overlook mistakes*
> *that have been given no effects."*
> —T.595; T-30.VI.10:2

By not being affected by *"sin"* we remove its cause. Jesus did not condemn those who crucified him. Our task is no different than his. There is no death and this we demonstrate by showing that we cannot be hurt. Don't teach others that they can hurt you. Teach them, rather, that their supposed guilt is the fabric of a senseless dream (T.256; T-14.III.8:2).

Perception of sin occurs within the dream world of the ego as it projects betrayal onto the world. When we discover that what we perceived as sin is a part of our ego's feeling hurt, it becomes possible to let it go.

Time and Forgiveness

Another way to say this is that time cannot intrude upon eternity, the unreal cannot affect the real. The ego by nature lives in time, constantly rehearsing the past and projecting the future. But if there is no past, then there is nothing to be hung up on. There is nothing to project onto. There is nothing to forgive. As a popular country and western song expresses it: "There is no future in the past."

> *"Forgiveness does not aim at keeping time*
> *but at its ending, when it has no use.*
> *Its purpose ended, it is gone.*
> *And where it once held seeming sway*
> *is now restored the function God established*
> *for His Son in full awareness."*
> —T.572; T-29.VI.4:5-6

For forgiveness to work there must literally be no past to hang on to. When missionaries first went to Labrador, they found that the Innu people had no word for forgiveness. So they made up a word, which in the local language was: *Is-suma-gi-jou-jung-naimer-mik*, literally meaning "Not-being-able-to-think-about-it-anymore."

It is interesting that the missionaries believed that they had to come up with a word for forgiveness. Maybe the Innu had no word for forgiveness because one was not needed. There is another story of a Christian missionary who asked a young Innu girl if she had made her peace with God, to which the girl replied: "I did not know there was any argument."

The task is not to have any argument.

> *"All forms forgiveness takes that do not lead away from anger,*
> *condemnation and comparisons of every kind are death."*
> —The Song of Prayer III 8:1

The task is to let go so completely that there is no memory of wrong because there is nothing in us to make the other wrong. Only the ego can hold a grievance. As we are not ultimately the ego, so we cannot ultimately hold a grievance.

> *"When you bury a mad dog,*
> *don't leave his tail above ground."*
> —Charles Spurgeon

There is nothing to forgive unless we believe there is. As we forgive by not condemning, we are freed of suffering. In this process we ourselves are healed. As we give we receive, as we forgive (by not making the error real) so are we forgiven. As we forgive, so do we remember our heavenly home.

When faced with attack, criticism, and condemnation, it is helpful to recognize the following:

1. Safety lies in defenselessness

Jesus on the cross is showing us that ultimately we must be defenseless. This is true on a soul level. It is true on all levels. Ultimately, we stand naked before God. There is no effective attack, blame, or defense to be offered before God against any person. Excuses don't work in Heaven and they don't work here either. To say that safety lies in defenselessness doesn't mean we should not protect our body if someone physically attacks us. True forgiveness does not mean permitting destructive behavior, letting others take advantage of us, or living under conditions we find unbearable. Forgiveness requires that we be kind to ourselves as well as to others. It does mean that we do not need to jump to the defense for every little insult that seems to come our way.

2. All attack is a call for help

Even if we think that someone has mistreated us, rather than jumping to the defense before we have even thought about what we are doing, can we not realize that that person has acted out of fear and ignorance? Can we not see mistakes as a call for help?

> *". . . you are merely asked to see forgiveness*
> *as the natural reaction to distress that rests on error,*
> *and thus calls for help.*
> *Forgiveness is the only sane response."*
> —T.593; T-30.VI.2:7-8

During the Korean War, a South Korean civilian was arrested by the communists and ordered shot. But when the young communist leader learned that the prisoner was in charge of an orphanage, he decided to spare him and to kill his son instead. So they shot the nineteen-year-old boy in the presence of his father.

Later the fortunes of war changed, and the young communist leader was captured by the United Nations forces, tried, and condemned to death. But before the sentence could be carried out, the South Korean whose son had been killed pleaded for the life of the communist, saying: "He was young, he really did not know what he was doing."

The United Nations forces granted his request, and the father took the murderer of his son into his own home. When someone is going crazy in our presence, that person does not know what he or she is doing. That person needs our help, not our attack.

3. We may have done what the accused has done

Whenever we feel tempted to accuse someone of being a sinner, it is helpful to ask ourselves if what that person has done is something we would accuse ourselves of doing. In the story of the woman taken in adultery, Jesus suggests that the one who is without sin should cast the first stone. Beginning with the eldest, they drop their stones and walk away. Jesus then turns to the woman and asks, *"Woman, where are your accusers?"* to which she says, *"Lord, there are none."* Jesus then replies,

> *"Neither do I condemn you, go and sin no more."*

It is interesting that it is the eldest who drops the first stone. The more we've been here the more we know we are not without error.

4. There are lessons to be learned

When we have difficulty with our brothers or sisters, it is helpful to listen carefully to the criticism they offer and suspend our own defensiveness long enough to allow ourselves the opportunity to see things differently (without defensiveness) — perhaps even the way the other sees things. It is worth our time to listen carefully whenever anyone has a criticism of us for even the smallest thing. Rather than immediately jumping to the defense, which is what the ego wants to do, listen carefully, trying to understand why this person is saying what he or she is saying. Is there a small grain of truth in what this person is saying?

Listen carefully: What are they saying? In some way do you agree? Is there some way you might change to make things better? Here is a real opportunity for insight if we are willing to look at it. This is the deeper meaning of doing unto others as we would have them do unto us. Look for the "glimmer of truth" in the lesson your brother or sister would have you learn.

> *"If you bring your gift to the altar,*
> *and there remember that your brother has aught against you,*
> *leave there your gift before the altar,*
> *go your way and first be reconciled to your brother,*
> *and then come and worship."*
> —Matthew 5:23

Only when we have relinquished our grievances can we worship in thankfulness and peace. Forgiveness transforms vision and enables us to see the world behind confusion and chaos.

5. No one can hurt us

Everyone to whom we offer healing returns it. Everyone we attack keeps the attack and holds it against us. The cost of giving is always receiving. God is the only Cause and God does not cause guilt. What is not of God cannot have power over us (T.256; T-14.III.8:1f).

We would never attack another unless we believed that person had somehow taken the peace of God from us. But no one can take the peace of God from us. If we give others the power to take the peace of God from us, it is we who have given them that power.

6. Forgiveness must be total

> *"Then Peter went up to him and said,*
> *'Lord, how often must I forgive my brother*
> *if he wrongs me?*
> *As often as seven times?'*
> *Jesus answered,*
> *'Not seven, I tell you, but seventy times seven.'"*
> —Matthew 8:21–22

There is no order of difficulty in miracles. We cannot forgive some people but not forgive others. There cannot be some things we forgive in someone but other things about that same person we cannot forgive.

> *"Salvation rests on faith*
> *there cannot be some forms of guilt*
> *that you cannot forgive."*
> —T.595; T-30.VI.7:7

Forgiveness is not something we do sometimes. To forgive seventy times seven means to forgive repeatedly, no matter how wrong we might think another has been, no matter how many times we may think we have been abused. The answer remains:

"Forgive," "Forgive," "Forgive."
"Let it go," "Let it go," "Let it go."

Aggression never succeeds. Jesus on the cross was denied and betrayed even by Peter. If there was ever someone who seemed to have a right to be indignant, it was Jesus. If Jesus had seen sin in his disciples, if he had made them wrong, if he had condemned them, it would have proven he was ego-bound, and not the Christ.

7. Forgiveness itself is an illusion

It may sound funny having said so much about forgiveness to now say that forgiveness itself is an illusion, but it is. Just as the Atonement is the only defense that does not lead to further defensiveness, so forgiveness is an illusion that does not lead to further illusion. It is an illusion because there is nothing to forgive in the first place. There is something to forgive only if we think there is something to forgive.

"Illusions make Illusion. Except one.
Forgiveness is illusion that is answer to the rest."
— W.369; W-198.2:8-10

Forgiveness is the end of dreaming because it is awakening. Forgiveness is not the truth but it points to where the truth is. Forgiveness leads us out of disaster, not into further disaster. Ultimately, once we have forgiven we see that no forgiveness was necessary; we just thought there was. What has really happened is that in the process of forgiving we have discovered who we really are. We have awakened to our own call. We have found our way home again.

Peace Is Obtainable

Peace is obtainable when we hold to these ideas:
1. Peace of mind, salvation, and the abundance that comes with it can be our only goal.

"Forgiveness is man's deepest need
and highest achievement."
—Horace Bushnell

2. Forgiveness is the key to salvation and peace of mind.

3. Through forgiveness we begin to see everyone, including ourselves, as guiltless. If Jesus on the cross can forgive murderers, can we not be more tolerant of lesser sins that we think have been committed against us?

4. As we give up our grievances we find ourselves becoming increasingly aware of the ever-present subtle and gentle guidance of Holy Spirit. Following Holy Spirit, we do not condemn others. It is then that we can experience peace of mind. With Holy Spirit's guidance, it becomes possible to know what we are supposed to do and do it.

- As long as we are unforgiving we can justify the belief that whatever is wrong in the world is outside or other than us.

- As long as we think there is something we cannot forgive we block our own way to the Kingdom.

- As long as we project guilt and sin upon the world, we ourselves live in confusion and despair.

- As long as we live in fear, love has no place in our hearts.

We came into this world with all we need and we can take it with us when we leave. There is nothing to fear. No one can take anything from us. To be alive, free, and at peace — forgive. Only as we forgive do we know ourselves the way God created us. Only as we forgive do we experience the Kingdom of Heaven.

"To be alive and not to know yourself
is to believe you are really dead."
—W.260; W-139.3:2

Jesus assures us that as we forgive, so are we forgiven. To forgive is to overlook, to relinquish the past, to let go of everything, to hold on to nothing. In the deepest sense to forgive means to forget, to forget where the hatchet is buried, to let it go to another time and go on.

Peace of mind occurs as we drop our concern with getting, drop the need to be right and concentrate on giving. Only then do we truly receive. Inner peace can be achieved only when we have forgiven. Forgiveness is the vehicle for changing our perception and letting go of our fears, condemnations, judgments, and grievances. It is helpful to give up the idea that someone has harmed us in any way.

There is nothing to forgive unless we think there is. If we think there is something to forgive, then we have chosen to make an error real. We teach our brothers and sisters that they cannot hurt us by not making error real.

"There is nothing to hold on to.
Nothing!"

Chapter 14

You Need Do Nothing

There is a Zen story about four students who decided to go into silence for a week. A few hours passed and one said, "I wonder if I remembered to turn off the stove."

Another said, 'You fool, you have spoken, and we agreed not to speak."

The third said, "What are you thinking? You have spoken too."

And the fourth said, "I am the only one who has not spoken."

The ego has great difficulty in being satisfied with what is. When we are not at peace there are many ways we can be dissatisfied or feel as though we must change things.

The question, says Hamlet, is "to be or not to be." But Buddha says that the question isn't a question at all — that the true path of contentment lies in "choicelessness" — in just letting things be. The *Course* says that while we may think of life as a journey, in fact there is no journey, only an awakening (T.222; T-13.II.7:3) — only a coming to ourselves as we already are. True contentment is found through letting ourselves and others be just who they and we are.

The Ego Is Always Choosing — Something Else

The ego is never quite content, never quite capable of living in the moment. Choose one thing and your ego will suggest you choose something else.

Eat too much and you start thinking how nice it would be to be thinner. Go on a diet and you will start thinking about food.

Become worldly and you start thinking about how nice it would be to be more spiritual. Become a monk and you start thinking about sex, money, talking, and freedom.

We want to be married. We get married and then start thinking how nice it would be to be single.

Overwhelmed with the city, we start thinking about the country. Go to a farm in Vermont and you start thinking about the excitement of life in the city.

We can't wait for vacation time to come. We start thinking about blue sky, green trees, mountain peaks, and forests. Go to the top of the mountain, look out at the beauty below, and soon you start thinking about being home.

I once knew a man who worked in a busy office at the World Trade Center. One day at a party, as we were sitting and talking in a relaxed sort of way, he began to tell me about his dream. He was leading a busy life in the city, but he wanted to be a small-town librarian. I wonder, if he had become a librarian would he have started to think about the World Trade Center?

I know an older man who is retired, with a nice income and a lovely home on which the mortgage is fully paid. Yet all he talks about is: "Will there be enough? Will the bills get paid?" The bills have always gotten paid. Yet he goes on worrying and misses what he has.

What we have, we miss. We have wonderful children who fill our lives. Yet we may miss the value and beauty of our own children. Live in a beautiful valley surrounded by mountains and you may never see the mountains.

At the time of my first encounter with the *Course* I was teaching a course on religions of the Far East: Buddhism, Taoism, Confucianism, and Shinto. I was interested in the philosophy of Taoism, because the path suggested a gentle approach to life. One of my favorite concepts from the *Tao Te Ching* is the idea of *wu-wei*, which literally means "do nothing." *Wu-wei* means quietism, nonaggression, nonmeddlesome action. Broadly, it means action not contrary to nature. Lao-tzu said that the Tao "does nothing." Tao is not a thing. Tao is never an object or a process. Tao has no opposites or polarities. Nothing came before Tao. Nothing made Tao. Yet through doing nothing all things are done. The Tao has great power because of its passivity.

The final goal of Taoism is the ecstasy of absorption into quietude and ultimate truth of the Tao. We cannot push our way into this ecstasy. It comes as we sit down, shut up, become quiet and receptive. The *Course* suggests that to find peace we need do nothing.

"Now you need but to remember you need do nothing.
It would be far more profitable now
merely to concentrate on this than to consider what you should do.
When peace comes at last to those who wrestle with temptation
and fight against the giving in to sin;
when the light comes at last into the mind given to contemplation;
or when the goal is finally achieved by anyone,
it always comes with just one happy realization;
'I need do nothing.'"
—T.363; T-18.VII.5:5-7

The realization that one need do nothing is a means of saving time. There is no manipulation of the universe, no changing of anyone else that needs to take place.

"I need do nothing
is a statement of allegiance, a truly undivided loyalty.
Believe it for just one instant, and you will accomplish more
than is given to a century of contemplation,
or of struggle against temptation."
—T.363; T-18.VII.6:7-8

To do anything involves the body, yet we have seen that we are not bodies. So the *Course* says:

"To do nothing is to rest,
and make a place within you
where the activity of the body ceases to demand attention."
—T.363; T-18.VII.7:7

We cannot find peace by fighting against sin. As long as we are fighting something, as long as there is a struggle, we must believe in the reality of that which we fight against and we cannot be at peace. "Muddy water let stand," says the *Tao Te Ching*, "will clear." Turbulence stirs up the mud. If not further churned up and interfered with, it settles down. So too our minds can come to clarity and peace.

Witnessing

Clarity and peace come through what Plato, Hegel, and Gurdjieff all called "witnessing." Witnessing is the ability to see without getting caught in the soap opera. Plato said a philosopher should be like a spectator at a sporting event. From the vantage point of a spectator you can see the events of the game. The players on the field see only part of the game. Their perspective is limited because they are enmeshed in the game. Our task is one of being able to watch what is happening on the playing field of our lives without getting caught up in the fray. When we get caught in the world we lose equilibrium and perspective. The capacity to witness frees us.

God is in control, and things change just fine without our pushing. Nothing needs to be forced. The Book of Ecclesiastes tells us that everything has its time and its season. Peaks are followed by valleys, highs are followed by lows, lows are followed by highs, successes by failures and failures by success.

Choicelessness

Life, says the *Tao Te Ching*, is fettered with is and is not. The more we cling, the more we are likely to exhaust ourselves or those to whom we cling. There is no need for clinging. Fears and jealousy are nonsense. No matter how grim any situation might appear, it is possible to see love through it — if we want to. Choicelessness, letting things be, is a way of getting away from clinging. Choicelessness is a way of stopping the world.

You've heard it said:

> *"You can fool some of the people all the time,*
> *and all of the people some of the time,*
> *but you cannot fool all of the people all of the time."*

I have another thought that is similar. If it isn't one of Murphy's Laws, it should be. It's one all teachers, waitresses, ministers — indeed anyone who must serve the public — will readily understand:

"You can satisfy some of the people all of the time,
all of the people some of the time,
but you cannot satisfy all of the people all of the time."

Trying to please everyone is not only very difficult, it is also very trying on the nerves.

The best procedure is to be true to oneself. We will then not satisfy all of the people, but we will satisfy many people. Most importantly we will find self-satisfaction. Some people may even be upset with us, but we need not get caught up in their upset nor attack them for it. Being true to ourselves, letting ourselves be, we can let others be. Jesus is a powerful example. Because he was entirely true to himself, many people were upset by him. But he was never upset because they were upset with him.

There is only one way you can ever be upset.
First you must have a set up.
There is only one way you can ever be disappointed.
First you must have an appointment
—an expectation about the way things should be.

Watch for the use of words like "upset," "disappointed," or "offended." It is a clear indication that our ego is plugged in. I was watching a well-known preacher on television. He said he would be very offended if he heard anyone use Jesus' name in vain. He might be offended, but Jesus is not going to get caught up in someone's little insult. Jesus knows who he is and is far beyond being bothered by a mindless insult. Someone once wisely said that you add as much strife to the world when you take offense as when you give it.

Beliefs

There are many ways to handle differences without argument. Jesus never entered into arguments. In reply to the Pharisees he simply spoke the truth. In light of his truth they either remained silent or got more defensive. But he did not enter into argument. To most of the challenges of the Pharisees he gave a reply that was so profound it left them speechless. There was no way to argue with him. Jesus didn't create an argument. In fact he says:

"Make friends quickly with your accuser,
while you are going with him to court,
lest your accuser hand you over to the judge,
and the judge to the guard,
and you be put in prison."
—Matthew 5:25

Each of us holds on to a separate set of beliefs. The dictionary says that beliefs are "ideas we hold about what is true or real." There are obviously many different belief systems and "ideas" about what is real or true. All of them cannot be true. Some of these ideas are in direct conflict with others.

The Old Testament says:

"An eye for an eye, a tooth for a tooth."

But Jesus says:

"Not an eye for an eye, but love your enemies,
and pray for those who persecute you."

In the same way, when we are in love in the true sense of what love means — not passion and attachment, but when we love someone unconditionally — we don't have to change that person. We love that person for who he or she is. If we can be together with differences, wonderful. If not, we can part with love and without attack.

Everyone likes to be right, but it is not necessary to be right. The *Course* asks us:

"Would you rather be right or happy?

The *Tao Te Ching* says

"Wanting to be right blinds people."

There is no reason to create a soap opera. There is no reason to try to manipulate others to our way of thinking. Our petty little ego concerns, or those of someone else, are not all that important. We agree or we don't. Find some way to cooperate or let it go. It isn't necessary to insist on getting our way. It's important not to try to change others whom we have deemed sinners.

> I would rather have peace of mind.
> than give you a piece of my mind.

To be fulfilled and satisfied it is helpful to recognize the abundance we already have. We already are. If we do not see that we already are, we cannot know abundance. We already are, and as creative, inspired human beings we will experience even more abundance than we do now. We don't have to become something we're not. We just need to let ourselves be and make room for who we are to flow into expression.

There is no judgment to be made. We do not have to make someone else over. There is no one to manipulate and nothing to do. Be you, and it will come to you. Go chasing and you will find that you chase a dream, and there will inevitably be failure and disappointment.

The *Course* tells us that we are in need of nothing but the truth (W.410; W.pII.251). There is nothing we have to do except to wake up — to realize who we already are. In truth we are one Self united with our Creator. We are children of God.

> There is no place we have to go,
> There is no teacher at whose feet we need to sit,
> There is no book we need to read.

The only thing required is an awakening to our own call and the realization of the truth of who we already are. There is deep peace in the simple realization that:

"I need do nothing."

Part III

All about Nothing: The Metaphysics of Miracles

Chapter 15

You Are Not a Body

*"You brought nothing into this world
and you can take nothing from it."*
—1 Timothy 6:7

*"All whom Moses calls wise are represented as sojourners. Their souls
are colonists leaving heaven for a new home. Their way is to visit
earthly nature as men who travel abroad to see and learn. So when
they have stayed awhile in their bodies and beheld through them all
that sense and mortality have to show, they may make their way back
to the place from which they first set out. To them the heavenly region
where their citizenship lies is their native land; the earthly region in
which they became sojourners is a foreign country."*
—Philo Judea (ca. 25 B.C.E.)

The Body

Some definitions of the body offered by thinkers of the past
include:

*"A thing of shreds and patches,
borrowed unequally from good and bad ancestors
and a misfit from the start."*
—Ralph Waldo Emerson

"Only a prison."
—Mohandas Gandhi

"A bundle of aches, longing for rest."
—Edna St. Vincent Millay

"An affliction of the soul . . . a burden, a necessity,
a strong chain, and a tormenting punishment."
—Palladas

"The tomb of the soul."
—Plato

"Not a home but an inn — and that only briefly."
—Seneca

According to the *Course* the body

"is the ego's chosen home . . .
merely part of our experience in the physical world."
—T.20; T-2.IV.3:8

"a means and not an end."
—T.386; T-19.IV.B.10:5

"outside you but seems to surround you."
—T.360; T-18.PVI.9:1

"a limit imposed on the universal communication
that is an eternal property of mind."
—T.360; T-18.VI.8:3

"the central figure in the dreaming of the world."
—T.543; T-27.VIII.1:1

"the great seeming betrayer of faith."
—T.386; T-19.IV.B.II:4

"a tiny fence
around a little part of a glorious and complete idea."
—T.364; T-18.VIII.2:5

"a limit on love."
—T.364; T-18.VIII.1:2

"the ego's chosen weapon
for seeking power through relationships."
−T.407; T-20.VI.4:3

"nothing."
−T.389; T-19.IV.5:5

The ego thinks of the body as reality, yet somehow we also know it is not home. The *Course* says the body is the thought of separation projected by the mind into form. This leaves us with confusion; somehow we know that we are not bodies, yet there is so much reinforcement that we are bodies.

Feeling that the body limited spirit, some of the early Gnostics and medieval mystics did everything they could to deny the body: they wore hair shirts, sat outdoors in inclement weather, flagellated themselves, and fasted to the point of death, all in an attempt to escape from the body while ironically making the body the primary object of their concern. On the other extreme there were the libertines who, also saying that the body had nothing to do with spirit, thought they could do anything they wanted and engage in bodily excess and extravagance.

The ego looks for security in the body and tries in every way it can to find the eternal through the body. We live in an age of glamor and fashion, of facelifts and cryogenics. We are easily fascinated with the body and our "visage." First thing each morning we go to the mirror and check out our reality as a body. We then clean it and try to make it as attractive as possible for other bodies to look at. If we are sick or we are overweight or feel ugly in some way, we may also hate the body, feeling that it is not good enough to be our home.

Knowing the body is not eternal, we look for compromises or pretend we will live forever. As our friend Rabbi Gelberman says jokingly about death: "I'm not going!" We may also try to create eternity in external objects and/or in other bodies as in children, books, art, and institutions. We build mausoleums for our bodies or have buildings and streets named after us all in the "grave" hope of some earthly immortality.

Appetites Come Not from the Body

"The spirit indeed is willing, but the flesh is weak."
—Matthew 26:41

However much we may want to blame the body, the *Course* says that lust does not come from the body. In fact, none of the so-called appetites is of the body.

"Appetites are 'getting' mechanisms,
representing the ego's need to confirm itself.
This is as true of the body appetites
as it is of the so-called 'higher ego needs.'
Body appetites are not physical in origin.
The ego regards the body as its home,
and tries to satisfy itself through the body.
But the idea that this is possible is a decision of the mind,
which has become completely confused about what is really possible."
—T.52, 53; T-4.II.7:5-9

It is important to know that everything that happens does so within the realm of the mind. Dr. Wapnick repeatedly points out that while we may think that the body is in charge and dictates to us, the mind, the decision-maker, is always in control. We've all heard how rape is not a result of sexual drive but of the mind of the rapist, who wishes to possess another.

Despite the fact that it is the mind that is at all times in control, probably all of us have felt at times that the body was the master of our lives. We confirm our bodily life whenever we overindulge in any physical activity—overeating, overdrinking, oversleeping. We are very easily addicted, and in trying to make the body more enjoyable we often satiate it with cholesterol, caffeine, chocolate, sugar, tobacco, alcohol, and drugs. We can even be addicted to and crave so-called good food. So when we choose our addictions we need to choose them well.

"No one is free who is a slave to the body."
—Seneca

Of all the areas in which we are confused and bewildered there is probably none more confusing than sexuality. Sexuality is clearly a bodily function. Most divorces are said to be over sexual incompatibility or disagreement about money. The incredible variety of men's magazines featuring nude women and the number of women's glamour magazines, along with tabloid newspapers and television shows, serve as testimony to our fascination with sexuality.

While we are here in this world, in these bodies, we tend to get very attached to them and even tend to think that we are our bodies. We have a great concern for the health of our bodies. We spend a tremendous amount of money on cosmetics and clothes and jewelry to adorn our bodies.

> *"Adornment of the body seeks to show*
> *how lovely are the witnesses for guilt.*
> *Concerns about the body demonstrate*
> *how frail and vulnerable is your life."*
> —T.526; T-27.I.6:9-10

To see how the ego uses the body, one need only to look at the innumerable ads for designer jeans, furs, and expensive dresses. Billions of dollars are spent annually on cosmetics. We spend billions on doctors, hospitals, and insurance. Think how different things would be if we did not seek to abuse the body or lock up our fears in our bodies. Don Juan of the Carlos Castañeda series says:

> *"Westerners deal with their bodies by filling them*
> *with alcohol, bad food, and anxiety,*
> *all of which keep them from seeing."*
> —Carlos Castañeda,
> *Journey to Ixtlán*, p. 62

The body is the ego's "proof" that the ego is real, that we are separate. On the one hand, the ego adorns and glorifies the body. On the other hand, it attacks the body to convince us we are frail and vulnerable.

According to the *Course* the body in and of itself is neutral. It is neither good nor bad. Good and bad come as the mind interprets the functions and actions of the body. The body may be a peaceful, helpful tool. As the central figure in the ego's dream of the world, the body may also be experienced as the very thing that separates us from God.

> *"The body is beautiful or ugly, peaceful or savage,*
> *harmful or helpful, according to the use to which it is put."*
> —T.140; T-8.VIII.4:3

The more we think of ourselves only as bodies the more confusing
the world.

> *"When you equate yourself with a body*
> *you will always experience depression."*
> —T.140; T-8.VII.1:6

When we are sick it seems pretty obvious that we are bodies, and
that is depressing. As the ego cannot conceive of itself as separate
from a body, the body becomes the symbol of the ego just as the ego
is the symbol of separation. As inhabiter of the body, the ego uses the
body for attack, pleasure, and pride. Overidentified with the body and
not knowing eternity, we are also afraid of the death of the body. Our
bodies grow old, wither, gasp a last time, and are laid in the ground
to decay. The ego uses this vulnerability of the body as an argument
for the nonexistence of God or as evidence that God is angry with us.
Such is the ego's view of the body.

The Body Cannot Die

At one point the *Course* says:

> *"at no single instant does the body exist at all."*
> —T.362; T-18.VII.3:1

On the surface of things this sentence does not seem to make
sense, for if there is one thing that seems obvious it is our bodies. But
you might notice right away that we say "our bodies" as though we are
the possessors of the body and not the body itself.

Let me suggest an analogy that may be helpful, namely, that not
for a moment does your car exist. We could take this further and say
that not even for a moment does the world exist, but we'll start with
a smaller object.

Now certainly the car — that is, a thing that is made of metal, that
has seats inside, a motor in front and wheels on four corners, and is

used for locomotion so that we can move our bodies around in this world—that object does *seem* to exist. We even talk about the "life of a car," meaning the number of years the car will be able to function until it is no longer capable of carrying us about.

French Jesuit priest Pierre Teilhard de Chardin felt that one of the definitions of life was that it was something that moved. He felt that all things had life, because all things are made up of atoms that themselves are made up of electrons and neutrons "moving" around in each other in space. Given that atoms move, they must have some "inner" energy that makes them move.

If we were looking at this earth through a gigantic telescope from a planet a great distance away, it might look as though there were "car-like beings" that move around the planet on paths that have been laid out for them. It would seem as though they move about with some meaningful and purposeful motion.

We might even notice a number of different "races," "clans," or "tribes" of cars.

We might notice the great variation in size and shape and apparent function.

We might notice certain special classes of cars that have the ability to fly through the air, float on the water, even swim underwater.

We might notice further that these cars "eat" or "drink" some sort of liquid that apparently gives them energy. At times they seem to rest. At some point they also seem to die.

Now when a car "dies"—when it is no longer capable of locomotion, when its usefulness is over and it no longer serves a purpose—a car is taken to a "graveyard" where in time it is put into a great crushing machine. The resultant block of metal is placed into a huge melting pot where the steel is separated from the aluminum, the dross is burned off, the remaining steel is mixed with other steel, and the whole thing gets recycled into a sheet of metal that may find its way back into another car. As a matter of fact, cars are the most recycled of all products.

The material thing in and of itself is not what constitutes life. Although we may in fact say, "My car died," we have no trouble understanding that the car itself was never really "alive" at all. Strange as the idea may seem, could it possibly be the same with our bodies?

We "drive" our bodies around for a while, and they too begin to age. I remember listening to Dr. Joseph Campbell talking about reaching old age; he said it was like having an old car. You begin to notice that the gears are shifting more slowly, a fender gets crumpled, the tailpipe begins to drag, and in general there is less get-up-and-go. Campbell described experiencing himself more and more as the consciousness that was animating a body and not as the body itself.

It is possible, of course, to keep our cars in good shape for a long time with proper care. We can replace dented fenders, get tune-ups, and improve the overall look and performance of the car.

In the same way we can have face lifts and other operations to improve the overall look of the body. And the length of time we spend in the body may well be correlative to the way we take care of it. We would not put lemonade in the gas tank of our cars and expect them to run very well. Neither would we put gasoline into our bodies and expect them to run very well. We have learned that there are certain lubricants that are better than others for the running of a car, just as there are certain foods that are better than others for the running of the body. It is perhaps surprising that some of us seem to give more or better attention to the proper health, care, and maintenance of our cars than we do to the maintenance of our bodies.

Once the usefulness of a car is over and it has been melted down again, you might ask: Did that car ever exist at all? It did *seem* to exist for a while. It even appeared to have a "brain." That is, there was something that made it go in one direction and then another. Once upon a time it seemed to have a life and now it no longer has it.

Once upon a time there was someone you think of as your great-great-grandfather. That being as a bodily being certainly does not exist any more. Indeed the carbon atoms that made up that body no longer exist as they once did. And it does not matter that they no longer exist.

Our bodies have no more life than do our cars. They simply represent temporary manifestations of highly complex forms of carbon that have the power of locomotion. Yet the *Course* says that life is not of the body. There is therefore no death, for that which was not alive in the first place cannot die.

> *"The body no more dies than it can feel.*
> *It does nothing.*

*Of itself it is neither corruptible
nor incorruptible.
It is nothing.
It is the result of a tiny,
mad idea of corruption that can be corrected."*
—T.389; T-19.IV.5:2-6

Our cars may appear to have a life. We might even give them names and develop emotional attachments to them. Yet the car never was or is alive. In the same way our bodies are not that which constitutes life. Life is of the spirit. For a little while, in this dream, Spirit seems to be driving around in or "trapped" in a body.

Looked at with bodily eyes, death is frightening, for it looks like the end. But there cannot be an end to that which had no beginning. Do dream characters exist outside of the mind of the dreamer? Do cartoon characters or fictional characters in a novel or movie really exist? Our assistant Ruth Murphy regularly brings her two-year-old son Kenny to work. Kenny often sits and watches cartoons while we work. He often speaks of cartoon characters as though they are alive. "Mommy, look at Barney!" As far as Kenny is concerned Barney and Pinky and Batley are real.

When I was a child I had a cloth doll named Joe, named for the boxer Joe Lewis. Joe still sits up on my bookshelf. As a child I thought Joe was alive. I still talk to Joe from time to time as though he were alive. At least I talk to the spirit of the doll who has loved me unconditionally for many years, but I know that there is no life in the material thing itself.

Several years ago I dated a woman who played a character on an afternoon soap opera. She told stories of how more than one person had written telling her to watch out for another character in the show because that character was out to get her. Somehow the people who wrote in thought her character was a real person.

It's easy to get caught up in the life of the body. It is easy to get caught in the life of the ego as though that life was somehow what's real. The *Course* tries to help us to see that there is indeed a real life, but it has nothing do with our bodies.

Ken Wapnick likes to use the analogy of a puppet to describe the body. If you watch a puppet moving around on a stage, it seems as though the puppet has life, yet we know that there is no life in the puppet. Someone is pulling the strings.

It is spirit that is alive — the only thing that really is alive — not the body itself. The mind, in the terms of the *Course*, is *the activating agent* of spirit.

You cannot die for there is only life. The carbon atoms that make up the body will one day be recycled into the earth as surely as the metal in our cars is recycled and turned back into steel. But nothing at all will have happened to *you*.

According to the *Course* the creations of God are not destructible. The body is obviously destructible. That which is eternal cannot be destroyed. While material objects clearly can be destroyed, Spirit cannot.

> *"The body is the symbol of what you think you are.*
> *It is clearly a separation device,*
> *and therefore does not exist."*
> —T.97; T-6.V.A.2:2

We Are Spirit

How do we know that we are spirit and not body? First of all, as a creation of God, what we are cannot be confined to something material that will rot, rust, decay, and be recycled. As Coleridge expressed it, the body is indeed "a house of clay."

Second, we do have a great power of intuition. In fact the *Course* suggests that as we come to the knowledge of the unreality of the body we must at the same time begin to develop certain "psychic" or intuitive abilities that enable us to see things that the body's eyes could never see.

Third, as we begin to lose our fascination with the material, we begin to understand the nature of our true reality as love comes more and more to fill our hearts. Love comes to fill our hearts as fear melts away. Our biggest fear is that we are going to die. But you can't die because there is only life. There is no such thing as death. The ego can disappear, but the ego was never anything more than a character in a dream. The ego cannot die because the ego never existed. In the

same way the body never exists, though within this illusion it "looks"
as though it does.

This is in no way to suggest that we should do away with our bodies, any more than we need to do away with our cars or computers or
other useful tools. We're here to learn, and we can't learn the lessons
we need to learn by dropping out of class.

> *"The Holy Spirit does not see the body as you do,*
> *because He knows the only reality of anything*
> *is the service it renders God*
> *on behalf of the function He gives it."*
> —T.140; T-8.VII.3:6

The body can also be, a *"link"* or *"tool,"* a connection between Self
and God.

> *"The body is a harp for the soul."*
> —Kahlil Gibran

According to the *Course*, the body is a communication medium
that receives and sends messages. In the hands of the ego, it communicates pain, fear, separation, despair, and anger. In the hands of Holy
Spirit, it communicates healing love, unity, and joy.

I have a friend who says I should stop telling people they are not
bodies. If I seem to be overstating the fact it is because we are so
overidentified with the body in the first place that only by pointing
in the completely opposite direction can we begin to find some middle
way to deal with the body. It is helpful to realize how bodily oriented
we are and how fascinated we are with the body in order to begin to
get another perspective and thus gain some freedom from the seeming tyranny of the body — which is really not of the body but of the
mind.

Ultimately we want to understand the body as does the Holy
Spirit.

> *"The Holy Spirit's picture changes not the body*
> *into something it is not.*
> *It only takes away from it all signs of accusation*
> *and of blamefulness.*
> *Pictured without a purpose,*

it is seen as neither sick nor weak, nor bad nor good.
No grounds are offered that it may judge in any way at all.
It has no life, but neither is it dead."
—T.527; T-27.I.9:3-7

When we live like Jesus we discover that we are ourselves Eternal Sons of God. It is only spirit that matters. Spiritual life makes us eternal — nothing else. Past the dream and the visage of the body, past the wigs, elevator shoes, and mascara is something that radiates us, thinks us, feels us — is us. It is the living Christ. The body is nothing. And:

"You are not a body.
You are free.
Be free today.
And carry freedom as your gift to those who still believe
they are enslaved within a body.
Be you free,
so that the Holy Spirit can make use
of your escape from bondage....
Let love replace fear through you."
—W.373; W-pI.199.7:2

Chapter 16

You Cannot Be Betrayed, Persecuted, or Crucified: The Message of the Crucifixion

One of the characteristics of the ego is its belief that not only is it possible to be separate from God but it is also possible to be betrayed, persecuted, and crucified by our brothers and sisters, thus increasing our sense of separation. The *Course* even talks about the wish we have to be unfairly treated (T.525; T-27.I.1:1). The ego would like to show the world that it has been unjustly treated. In fact, the stance of the ego is often the position: "Behold me, brother; at your hand I die."

The ego is by nature on the defensive, taking the position that "other people are out to get me so I had better watch out and get mine while I can."

> *"You have probably reacted for years*
> *as if you were being crucified.*
> *This is a marked tendency of the separated,*
> *who always refuse to consider*
> *what they have done to themselves."*
> —T.85; T-6.I.3:1-2

You can probably think of individuals you know who repeatedly find trouble in their interpersonal relationships. It is often also obvious that these individuals bring difficulties upon themselves. Yet they invariably project the belief that they are not themselves responsible for the misfortune that seems to befall them.

If we act as though we are persecuted, then we must project the thought that someone else is unloving while we are the good person. All the while there is an underlying feeling of guilt, for underneath we know that we are projecting a false image to the world.

> *"My brothers and yours are constantly engaged*
> *in justifying the unjustifiable."*
> −T.87; T-6.I.11:4

The *Course* says that it is not "will for life" but "wish for death" that is the motivation of this world. From this standpoint it is the purpose of this world to prove that guilt is real — that other people can hurt us, betray us, persecute us, even crucify us.

Those who see themselves as persecuted not only place a burden of guilt upon themselves, they also try to ensnare their brother or sister in their guilt.

> *"You cannot crucify yourself alone."*
> −T.525; T-27.I.1:5

We have all, no doubt, acted at times as though someone else were responsible for how we feel. We have tried to make someone else feel guilty for the misfortunes we see coming our way. The *Course* says: *"A sick and suffering you but represents your brother's guilt."* (T.525; T-27.I.4:3) If we try to make someone else feel guilty, we seek to imprison that person along with us. Yet the truth remains. No one is responsible for how we feel except ourselves alone.

> *"Whenever you consent to suffer pain,*
> *to be deprived, unfairly treated or in need of anything,*
> *you but accuse your brother of attack upon God's Son."*
> −T.525; T-27.I.3:1

Jesus was whipped, beaten, and placed on a cross to die, yet he never condemned his accusers nor saw himself as crucified.

> *"Christ left us an example that we should follow in his steps.*
> *He did not sin, neither was guile found in his mouth.*
> *When he was reviled, he reviled not again,*
> *when he was tortured, he retaliated not*
> *but committed himself to Him that judges righteously."*
> −1 Peter 2:21

Jesus did not see himself as persecuted but saw only a call for help coming from those who attacked him. He did not look down from the cross and say:

> *"Look, you guys,*
> *I really am the Son of God,*
> *you are making a big mistake here,*
> *and, boy, are you in trouble!"*

Throughout Jesus' trial and crucifixion, he never offered any defense for himself. When he was standing before Pontius Pilate, and Pilate asked him if he had anything to say in his defense, he said nothing. To have had a defense would have been to have given in to the ego, and Christ cannot give in to the ego, for Christ is the very antithesis of the ego. Jesus never saw himself as betrayed. Neither can anyone be betrayed. Others may choose to misperceive who you are and project against you, but that has nothing to do with who you really are — or with who they really are.

Jesus did not condemn the disciples for their misperceptions; neither should we condemn others because they act out of ignorance. When others act out of ignorance and fear, they simply do not know who they are. As my old teacher of transpersonal psychology, Dr. Thomas Hora, used to say: "Ignorance is not a person."

The Church's View of the Crucifixion

For the early Christians the fish was the symbol for Christianity. The fish lives in water, as the Christian was to live by baptism. The fish in the story of the miraculous feeding of the five thousand became a symbol of the Christ who was able to feed everyone. Furthermore, the Greek word *Ichthus* is composed of the first letters of the words "Jesus Christ God's Son Savior." Yet over the course of history, the cross — a reminder of torture and death — replaced the fish as the primary symbol of Christianity. In the Catholic Church, it is not just the cross but the crucifix with the bleeding, dying Jesus upon it that stands as the symbol of Christendom.

On the surface, the crucifixion of Jesus looks like a horrible event. It seems clear that Jesus suffered, bled, and died "for our sins" — according to traditional Christianity. The church has placed a great deal of emphasis on the suffering of Jesus, for it appears as though he were the victim of the ego's cruelty. There is a church in a town near our home that proudly displays a sign in front of the sanctuary that reads: "We preach Christ crucified." Indeed, many churches "preach Christ crucified."

At a Lenten workshop for Christian ministers that I attended many years ago the group leader gave spike nails to each participant so we could contemplate the suffering of Christ. He proceeded to describe in graphic detail how horrible the suffering of Jesus must have been. From this traditional standpoint the crucifixion is seen as the "witness" to the reality of suffering, sacrifice, and death that the world seems to demand of us.

The crucifixion, in Jesus' own eyes, was not a punishment. You can think of yourself as being punished only if you feel guilty. Jesus knew his guiltlessness, so there was no need or reason for a perception of punishment. He could not change the fact that others misperceived who he was. There were many who knew who he was and were there to support him, but there were many more who were frightened by him and, out of their fear, sought to do away with him.

The crucifixion of Jesus is an extreme example that teaches that our true Identity as Love can never be destroyed, for death has no power over life. Who we are, who we really are, cannot be persecuted. You are a son or daughter of God. God's children cannot be persecuted. As the line from Martin Luther's hymn "A Mighty Fortress" expresses it: "The body they may kill, God's truth abideth still; His kingdom is forever."

Beyond Assault

"Assault can ultimately be made only on the body.
There is little doubt that one body can assault another,
and can even destroy it.
Yet if destruction itself is impossible,
anything that is destructible cannot be real."
—T.85; T-6.I.4:1-3

This reflects Plato's idea that the Ideal Forms are the only things that are real and therefore indestructible. Obviously the body can be assaulted, but time and again the *Course* reminds us that we are not bodies — in part because bodies are destructible and you, the ultimate you that you really are, are indestructible. That does not mean that we should abuse our bodies, or allow others to take advantage of our bodies, or put our bodies in risky situations, or seek martyrdom. Jesus does not ask us to be martyrs but rather teachers of peace. The *Course* says the crucifixion was:

> *"the last useless journey the Sonship need take"*
> —T.85; T-6.I.2:6

> *"You are not persecuted, nor was I.*
> *You are not asked to repeat my experience*
> *because the Holy Spirit,*
> *Whom we share, makes this unnecessary."*
> —T.87; T-6.I.11:1-2

If we know who we are — if we are clear about our identity as a child of God — then we know that we cannot be assaulted. We cannot experience persecution unless we see ourselves as persecuted. The ego is fragile; it feels hurt and is easily abused. One little word improperly placed, or even the wrong intonation or emphasis, and there we go, spinning off in thoughts of betrayal and persecution.

I once watched a "bang, bang, shoot'em up, get in the cars and chase each other" television show and noticed that all either the good guys or the bad guys had to do to get a fight started was to say something about the other guy's mother.

Do you know who your mother is? Why would you take it personally if someone were to insult your mother by saying something that was not true? Why feel persecuted by it? Why attack the other? The ego is often silly. Isn't it the truth that matters? Isn't it the truth that we are after? A lie does not change the truth.

> *"You are free to perceive yourself as persecuted if you choose.*
> *When you do choose to react that way, however,*
> *you might remember that I was persecuted as the world judges,*
> *and did not share this evaluation for myself."*
> —T.-85; T-6.I.5:2-3

Seeing Attack Another Way

When people act as though they have been persecuted, you can see that their reaction is coming from fear. Jesus asks us to see attack in a wholly different way. The *Course* tells us that *"as we teach, so do we learn."* If we react as if we are persecuted, we teach persecution. But you — who you really are — cannot be persecuted. Only the ego can be persecuted, and you are not an ego.

> *"Rather, teach your own perfect immunity,*
> *which is the truth in you,*
> *and realize that it cannot be assailed.*
> *Do not try to protect it yourself,*
> *or you are believing that it is assailable."*
> —T.85; T-6.I.5:4-5

Again, this does not mean that we should not protect our body if it is assaulted. We are talking about the level of our minds, not the level of form, about how we perceive an event, not how we respond to it behaviorally.

If Jesus could hang on the cross — his body bleeding and dying, a jeering crowd yelling at him — and not see himself as persecuted, can we not believe that we could see differently in the less extreme situations in which we perceive attack as coming our way?

All we are asked to do is to follow his example in much less extreme cases.

All we are asked to do is to teach only love in each and every situation, including the times when we seem to be persecuted.

If you can change your mind in such a situation and realize that the other is coming at you in fear instead of love, then you know you do not have to get caught in fear yourself. This is a miracle.

Resurrection is an awakening from the nightmarish thinking in which we see ourselves as persecuted. The crucifixion cannot be shared because it is a form of projection, but the resurrection, the symbol of reawakening, can be shared. The Atonement, by definition, must be shared. This is the good news: there is no victory in death and crucifixion. There is great victory in recognizing one's innocence, eternity, and wholeness.

The message of the crucifixion is: that it is not necessary to perceive any form of assault as persecution.

The message of the crucifixion is:

> *"You cannot be hurt,*
> *and do not want to show your brother anything*
> *except your wholeness."*
> —T.75; T-5.IV.4:4

The message of the crucifixion is: that you are beyond persecution and crucifixion.

You are in truth much bigger than that which can be crucified. Look not to the crucifixion but to the resurrection, for the resurrection gives life.

The Holy Spirit asks us to give a picture of ourselves in which there is no suffering, no pain, and no reproach at all. Our function is to show our brothers and sisters that their supposed sin has no cause and no effect.

Once we no longer project our guilt onto others, then it is possible to remember Heaven and return home once again. Let the message we give others be:

> *"Behold me, brother, at your hand I live."*
> *"Walk you the gentle way,*
> *and you will fear no evil and no shadows in the night."*
> —T.525; T.27.I.1:3

Chapter 17

There Is No Death

"Those who die before they die
don't die when they die."

You may know that Thomas Jefferson edited his own version of the Bible. Using a cut-and-paste method, he took out references to the supernatural and left in the moral teachings of Jesus. Jefferson's account of the story of Jesus ends with the sentence:

"There laid they Jesus and rolled a great stone
at the mouth of the sepulcher and departed."

Fortunately, that is not the end of the story. Because the Easter story does not end at the grave, we celebrate not death but life eternal.

Every year thousands of people climb a mountain in the Italian Alps passing the "stations of the cross" to stand at an outdoor crucifix. One day a tourist noticed a little trail that led beyond the cross. He struggled through the overgrown thicket and, to his surprise, came upon another shrine that symbolized the empty tomb. It was neglected. The brush had grown up around it. Almost everyone had gone as far as the cross, but there they stopped. If you stop at the cross, the message of Jesus' life is one of despair and heartbreak. You have to go beyond the cross to find the empty tomb.

We read in the Bible that on the morning of the third day Mary Magdalene and Martha went to the tomb of Jesus to put oil and spices on his body. When they found the tomb open, they concluded that the body had been stolen. Mary, meeting Jesus in the garden, believed him to be the gardener and subtly accused him of theft.

Every account we have of the Easter story confirms that the followers of Jesus were overwhelmed by the crucifixion and resurrection. Jesus had told them of the miracle that was to be. They had heard what he had to say, but no one understood what was happening. Now, with the open tomb in front of them, they did not know what to believe. Many thought his body had been stolen. Two thousand years later we are still trying to understand this event.

What Happened to Jesus?

Though there is no mention of it in the *Course,* on October 2, 1976, Helen asked Jesus what happened and received this answer:

> *"My body disappeared because I had no illusions about it.*
> *It was laid in the tomb but there was nothing left to bury.*
> *It did not disintegrate because the unreal cannot die.*
> *It merely became what it always was.*
> *And that is what 'rolling the stone away' means.*
> *The body disappears and no longer hides what lies beyond.*
> *To roll the stone away is to see beyond the tomb, beyond death,*
> *and to understand the body's nothingness.*
> *What is understood as nothing must disappear."*
> —Dr. Kenneth Wapnick,
> *Absence from Felicity,* pp. 398–99

Another way to talk about what happened can be found in the *Course,* when it says:

> *"There is either a god of fear or One of Love."*
> —M.63; M-27.4:6

Either there is death or there is life. From the standpoint of the ego, death is the final witness to the reality of the body. If the body dies, it must have lived — which means its creator, the ego, must be real as well.

If there is only life, then death of the body is not death. It is simply the quiet laying down of the body and the transformation from a dream of death to an awareness of eternal life. The meaning of Easter is that death is not real. Only the body disappears and the body isn't who we are in the first place.

"When your body and your ego and your dreams are gone,
you will know that you will last forever.
Perhaps you think this is accomplished through death,
but nothing is accomplished through death,
because death is nothing.
Everything is accomplished through life,
and life is of the mind and in the mind.
The body neither lives nor dies,
because it cannot contain you who are life."
—T.96; T-6.V.A.1:4

Jesus did not believe in death. He did not resist the crucifixion because he knew it meant nothing. He went to the cross to show us that while his body could be killed, that said nothing about who he was. The soul, which by definition is life, cannot be killed. Jesus knew he was eternal. What is true for him is true of us all.

"If we share the same mind,
You can overcome death because I did."
—T.97; T-6.V.A.1:5

The Resurrection

Easter is the decisive event in Christian history because it shows:

- *the victory of spirit over ego,*

- *of truth over falsehood*

- *of eternity over time.*

Christmas is no doubt the biggest holiday because of the materialism that surrounds it. Christmas celebrates the birth of a body, but birth into a body is a limitation in form. The ancient Greeks used to have a saying — *soma sema* — "the body is a tomb." If we see ourselves as bodies only then we cannot get beyond the delimited form of the body. Fortunately, our fears are groundless. The Easter story assures us that death is a lie. There is no death because there is only life.

Easter is a story of letting go. It is a story of freedom from illusion. The message of Easter is that we have nothing to lose, not even our bodies. To lose a body is just to lose a body. Death of the body is not the end. It's not the beginning. It is a continuing.

Krishnamurti says death is no big deal. It is birth into this world we should be concerned about. Jesus in the crucifixion and resurrection shows us that the body does not contain reality. Spirit cannot be limited to a specific experience in space and time.

> *"If the story of the wandering Jew be true,*
> *indeed if there was a man who could not die,*
> *would he not be the unhappiest of men?"*
> —Søren Kierkegaard

My encounter with death was an awakening. It was a coming back to life, not losing life. It was a raising of consciousness, not a loss of consciousness. It was as though I had been asleep and suddenly awoke. Nothing was lost except the dream.

Only the fearful dream disappears, only the ego and its attachments, hates, and prejudices. Only those things die that have no reality. Truth is, they don't even die; they just disappear into the nothingness of which they are already a part. Just like a dream, once it is gone, it is gone. Illusions never were part of eternity and never can be. Our prejudice, fear, and hatred are all part of an illusion; they will disappear because they have no truth in them, no eternity, no reality.

> *"Nothing real can be threatened."*

The resurrection is the triumph of Christ over the ego, not through any attack upon the ego but through a transcending of it. Jesus saw that there was a better way, a higher way of looking at the world. He knew the world was a place of transition and illusion, so it was easy to let it go.

Jesus in the Gospels says *"I am the vine, you are the branches."* As we come to live in Christ and he in us, we see that we cannot die because Christ cannot die. The proof of Christ's victory over the grave is that he lives in us today not as frivolous little egos, but as beings who are fully aware of our Identity as children of God.

In the early 1930s Communist leader Nikolay Bukharin journeyed from Moscow to Kiev to address a huge assembly. His topic was atheism. For over an hour and a half he laid out his fatalistic arguments.

At last he was finished, and religious faith, it seemed, was left smoldering in ashes. "Are there any questions?" he said. A large solitary man rose and asked permission to speak. He mounted the platform. Leaning over the podium, he slowly looked from left to right around the room. Then he shouted the ancient Orthodox greeting, *"Christ is risen!"* En masse the vast assembly arose, and the response came crashing like the sound of an avalanche:

"He is risen indeed!"

Only the fearful ego (which has nothing to do with who we are) can ever die — because (though it may sound strange) it never was! It exists only in a dream. It never meant anything. Ego life is part of the peripheral — the play, the game, a part of a dream that is only a crust to the Kingdom within.

Awakening begins as we realize we could dream a happy dream in which we realize that this body, this ego, this illusory world, is not all there is. In fact, it is nothing in light of the reality of God. To be truly awake means not to dream at all. It means to have no illusions, no fears or anxieties, only an awareness of eternal reality. Christ need not dream, for he lives in awakened reality. To share his reality is to be awake.

The Vision of Christ

To share in the Vision of Christ is to see Christ in everyone. It means to love others by letting them be who they are. As we get on with fulfilling our own destiny, we help others to fulfill theirs. Jesus got on with his destiny by going to the cross. Through the crucifixion and the resurrection he opened the door by which we might fulfill our destinies. He made clear the way to eternal life by distinguishing what is real from what is illusion. To see that, we must see:

"The door of the tomb is open! He is not here!"

Only spirit is. The body is gone because it meant nothing. It was only the form. You are not form but essence. Easter is the experience in which truth comes to the fore. We have only to speak the truth to gain entry into Heaven. The truth is simple and can be easily spoken.

At the gate, when asked your identity, say simply that you are a child of God.

The resurrection is the Will of God, which knows no time and no exceptions. To love oneself is to open the door to the effective love of others. To exclude anyone from the Kingdom of God is to exclude oneself.

We open the door to Heaven as we step aside and enable others to enter. In the crucifixion and resurrection is left behind everything that hurts, humbles, and frightens.

Easter
is the overcoming of death.
It is reawakening — rebirth.
it is a change of mind about the meaning of the world.

Easter
is the glad awareness of the Holy Spirit in our lives;
the recognition of the gifts of God;
the leaving of the past.

Easter
is the giving of the moment fully unto itself;
the lesson in which learning ends;
the relinquishing of all goals save God's.
There is no death, because dying means nothing.
Easter is the awareness of what already is.
It is the denial of death. It is the assertion of life.
The message of Easter
is that forgiveness is real.
Resurrection is the symbol of joy.
It represents what we all want to be.
Easter is a time of joy,
a time of peace, not pain.
It is a time of salvation.
It is the glad refrain,
the Son of God was never crucified.
—T.396; T-20.1, paraphrase

Chapter 18

There Is No World

And when he was demanded of the Pharisees, when the Kingdom of God should come, he answered them and said, "The Kingdom of God comes not with observation: Neither shall they say, Lo here! or, lo there! for, behold, the Kingdom of God is within you."
—Luke 17:20–21

One of the more difficult concepts in the *Course* is that there is no world. What do you mean, there is no world? Obviously there is a world: all we have to do is to look around and see it. Yet we read:

"There is no world!
This is the central thought this course attempts to teach."
—W.237; W-pI.132.6:2-3

This is the central thought that the *Course* would teach because the whole of the ego's structure is based upon the belief that the world, with all of its fears and anxieties, its pain and suffering, is real.

What Saying "There Is No World" Does Not Mean

To say there is no world does not mean that the *Course* makes the same mistakes as some of the early Gnostics. Seeing that the world was not real, some of the Gnostics engaged in a denial of the world and its influence in their lives.

To say there is no world does not mean that we can do whatever we want in this world without consequence. Indeed the *Course* teaches that not only do all of our actions have consequences in our experience but also that all of our thoughts have their effect.

To say there is no world does not mean that we should not enjoy or appreciate the beautiful mountains, rivers and forests, flowers and animals, good food and sexuality. My own earliest pull into exploring spiritual matters came in my experience of what might be called nature mysticism, and that is no doubt true for millions. But having said that, we still need to go deeper in our understanding.

The task is not to deny the world or hate the world or pretend we are not here. If we hate the world, then we make the world very real. Our task is to realize that we are making up the world and our interpretation of it.

1. There is no world because the world we see is whatever we make it to be

We talk about your world or my world or the world of the ancient Egyptians or the world of the Spanish conquistadors, realizing that each age and culture, even indeed each individual, has a different perspective on what the world is or was.

> *"The world is nothing in itself.*
> *Your mind must give it meaning."*
> —W.236; W-pI.132.4:1-2

The world we see is what we make it, nothing more. Because the world is what we are making it to be, and because we have made this place one of fear rather than love, the world is not what God created.

> *"There is no world apart from what you wish,*
> *and herein lies your ultimate release."*
> —W.236; W-pI.132.5:1

2. There is no world because there is no world apart from our idea about the world

The *Course* teaches that ideas leave not their source. We think the world is real because we are always making up the world. We are always dreaming the world.

> *"The world is but a dream that you can be alone,*
> *and think without affecting those apart from you."*
> —T.562; T-28.VII.5:2

If we saw the world the way God does, if we were capable of what the *Course* calls the Vision of Christ, then we would look upon the world with only love. If we looked upon this world with no fear in our hearts we would not see this world; we would see Heaven. Heaven is our only reality.

3. There is no world because God's world (Heaven) transcends time and space

I understand that there is no world in part because of my encounter with death. For a moment, I was able to attain to a different perspective. As I described it in first writing about the experience:

> Time started to collapse in a series of violent jerks. My life, my past, all was dying, turning to dust, disappearing. For a moment I remembered my father, my life on the farm, and that oh-so-ordinary reality which seemed like a space of bliss. I felt the most incredible sense of connection with the earth and that man. I then experienced what might be called the severing of the genetic-ego. The earth and every aspect of it flashed before me, was burned into a tiny crisp and disappeared in a zig-zagging line which now delineated a new universe. There was nothing left with which I could identify.

There was nothing left with which I could identify as an ordinary ego, as a person who lives in this world filled with ego anxieties — regrets, nostalgia, remorse, thoughts of sin, guilt, fear, etc. After this experience I was surprised to read the following in the *Course:*

> *"But healing is the gift of those who are prepared to learn*
> *there is no world, and can accept the lesson now.*
> *Some see it suddenly on point of death, and rise to teach it.*
> *Others find it in experience that is not of this world,*
> *which shows them that the world does not exist*
> *because what they behold must be the truth,*
> *and yet it clearly contradicts the world."*
> —W.237; W-pI.132. 7:1, 3, 4

Every now and then someone describes an experience that is not of this world. Certainly this is true for the descriptions of the mystics. Mystical experiences are so incredible that this world fades and pales in front of the experience.

One of the most interesting aspects of my experience was this zig-zagging line that delineated a new universe. This world appeared before me, then disappeared in a zig-zagging line. When the world disappeared there appeared in its place a multidimensional, multicolored grid, which is very difficult to describe in ordinary human words simply because there was an added dimension that is not comprehensible in a three-dimensional form. As words are but symbols of symbols and thus twice removed from reality, it is very difficult to put into words something that defies words. How do you describe another dimension?

4. There is no world because the world is temporal; Heaven is eternal

One of the things that struck me about my experience was the sense I had that we have all already seen what I saw. The experience suggested a confirmation of something Plato talked about twenty-four hundred years ago. In the *Meno*, the *Phaedo*, and the *Republic*, he put forth his theory of "recollection." Plato says our task in life is a matter of "re-membering," putting back together again what the soul already knows. This "re-collection" has nothing to do with this world. It is another world we need to remember.

It is interesting that other people who have had near-death experiences and mystical experiences also describe this colored grid. This grid, with its zig-zagging line, was somehow more real than this world. It seemed like a world I'd been to before. It was as if I were returning to reality, not losing reality.

5. There is no world because the world is in the past

"This world was over long ago."
—T.547; T-28:1:6

Think for a moment about your childhood. Does your childhood not seem like a dream, something that happened once upon a time, a very long time ago, in a distant land, in another world a long way from here? Imagine what it would be like if you left this world completely. What if you no longer had this body and all the things that identify it, all the accouterments of personality, of things and people who now surround you and give you definition. What would it be like if there were no such definition? Would it not seem like your former life had been a dream? And if it was a dream and the world now in front of you is more real than the dream, then would your focus not be on the world now before you and not upon the past? Most of us quickly forget our dreams, even those that are quite vivid and "seemingly" real. We forget our dreams and let them go because: "it was only a dream."

"There is a place in you where this whole world has been forgotten;
where no memory of sin and of illusion lingers still."
—T.570; T-29.V.1:1

Only that which is eternal lasts into eternity. Love is eternal, so love lasts. The ego is not eternal, so the ego cannot last.

To say there is no world is hard to accept because the world seems obvious. Yet once we leave it, it is gone. Once it is behind us, it is gone. The world exists in time. Heaven is not part of time. It is where we always have been.

No one has to accept this idea. The *Course* is always gentle. It leads along a path of peace, not a path of destruction. Our path is determined in each and every moment as we choose to be on guard with the ego or let go through love.

> *"Each one must go as far as he can let himself be led . . .*
> *He will return and go still farther,*
> *or perhaps step back a while and then return again."*
> —W.237; W-132.6:4-5

Life in this world is a constant process of stepping forward and then back again, of learning ever deeper lessons. We may rest awhile, then learn a deeper lesson yet again. When we choose from the framework of ego, we inevitably make wrong choices and are forced to learn through our mistakes. When we choose from the framework of Self — from our true identity as spirit — we cannot but make right choices and see the truth more clearly than ever before.

6. There is no world because there is no separation

> *"The world you see is based on 'sacrifice' of oneness."*
> —T.504; T-26.I.2:1

The world as we have created it is a place of separation, a place of sadness, sin, sickness, and suffering. The Bible says that when Adam and Eve bit into the apple and this world came into being, their eyes were opened and they knew good from evil. Suddenly there was a split, a separation. There is no world because the world is a place in which separation is made real, the ego is made real, the body is made real.

> *"Nothing in this world can give this peace,*
> *for nothing in this world is wholly shared."*
> —T.249; T-13.XI.4:1

The *Course* says that God's creations are unlike the world in every way. That is true because in God's creations there is no body; thus there is also no suffering, no pain, no loss, no separation, no death. There is nothing that this world holds that is valuable and real. In this world illusions hold sway while Heaven seems like a dream. Just the opposite is true. Heaven is real and this world a dream.

The *Course* says that the only purpose of the world is to prove guilt real (T.526; T-27.I.6:4). However disguised, this is always how the ego sees the world and why it would have us hold on to it. The Holy Spirit, God's Answer to the ego, sees the world as a place for us to learn forgiveness, a place to learn that guilt is not real and can have no real effects. To be free of the world and our attraction to it, we must forgive the world for all the things we think the world has done to us.

"When you forgive the world your guilt,
you will be free of it."
—T.546; T-27.VIII.13:2

God did not kick Adam and Eve out of Heaven. We left on our own accord. We took our talents and now are trying to make it on our own. We are all prodigal sons. Our Father is ever ready to receive us home again. In His eyes it does not matter what we have done or what we think we have done; all that matters is that we be willing to return home.

7. There is no world because there is only Heaven

While theologians quibble over various aspects of the teachings of Jesus, there is nearly universal agreement about his teachings concerning the Kingdom of Heaven. New Testament scholar Norman Perrin says that the Kingdom of Heaven is the central teaching of Jesus. All else in His message and ministry serves a function in relation to this proclamation and derives meaning from it. Every parable in the Gospel of Matthew begins with the phrase *"The Kingdom of Heaven is like...."* Clearly, Jesus wants us to know what the Kingdom of Heaven is like. In the Aramaic of Jesus' day, "kingdom" meant not a place but an act of God in which divine action is manifest. Kingdom means power and deed. It is the activity of God.

Where Heaven Is

The Kingdom of Heaven is central to who we already are at our very best. Its location? Jesus is very specific. He says it is within you. If the Kingdom of Heaven is within us, why don't we see it? We don't see it because we *are* it. We are standing in the middle of it, looking out on another world we believe to be more real than the Kingdom within.

> *"It is hard to understand what*
> *'The Kingdom of Heaven is within you' really means.*
> *This is because it is not understandable to the ego,*
> *which interprets it as if something outside is inside,*
> *and this does not mean anything.*
> *The word 'within' is unnecessary.*
> *The Kingdom of Heaven is you."*
> —T.54; T-4.III.1:1-4

We often feel estranged in this world, as though we are away from home.

> *"If I find in myself a desire*
> *which no experience in this world can satisfy,*
> *the most probable explanation is that*
> *I was made for another world."*
> —C. S. Lewis

We are all made for another world, because we are of another world. We live within the world of our individual soap operas. When reason rather than insanity guides our lives, we then "see" on a far deeper level. Then it is that we know we are not just egos trapped in finite bodies, but we actually see something more — something spiritual and divine.

> *"Everything you perceive as the outside world*
> *is merely your attempt to maintain your ego identification,*
> *for everyone believes that identification is salvation."*
> —T.206; T-12.III.7:5

Many of the meditative practices of the world's religions are specifically designed to help us see the Kingdom of Heaven by turning within. Meditation helps to shut down the exterior in order to see the interior. Living in the obvious world, we miss out on the subtle world of God. People who meditate become peaceable people precisely because they attain glimpses of the Kingdom within and thus know there is nothing outside themselves that can really be distracting.

Seeing the subtle Kingdom within enables us to live here better. When you know that Heaven is inside you and you look at something in the world that the ego would call bad, you know you do not have to get caught in it. Hell is the belief that we are caught in outer circumstances from which there is no escape. When you know that Heaven is inside, when you see the world the way Jesus or St. Francis did

> you can see craziness and not go crazy;
> you can see hatred and not hate;
> you can see sickness and not yourself get sick.

When we do not know that Heaven is inside us, then it is easy to go crazy, to get angry or off-center. Heaven is within us in that our True Self is within us. To come to Heaven is to come to ourselves. It is as the parable of the prodigal son tells us — a coming home, a returning to God.

The Gate of Heaven

If you believe Heaven is inside you, you can see it. If you don't believe it, it remains hidden. Heaven has nothing to do with the illusions of this world. Neither can we enter Heaven with illusions. To see Heaven we need to share in the Vision of Christ.

> *"I and the Father are One."*
> —Jesus

> *"Heaven means to be one with God."*
> —Confucius

Jesus so fully identified with God that he lived in Heaven while in this world. Most of us come here and are lost in guilt. Jesus came here like the rest of us but did not succumb to any of the temptations of the devil (ego).

The Kingdom already is. It is going to happen and it already is. The Kingdom is coming when we are yet trapped in ego structures. It already is for those who participate in it and understand it to be their natural inheritance. Pontius Pilate asked Jesus if he was a king and Jesus said,

> *"Yes, but my Kingdom is not of this world."*

God's Kingdom is not of the ego — the obvious and exterior. It has nothing to do with our story lines. Insofar as we live in personal dramas of our own making we know little of the Kingdom of God.

> *"This world is not the Will of God,*
> *and so it is not real.*
> *Yet those who think it real*
> *must still believe there is another will,*
> *and one that leads to opposite effects*
> *from those He wills."*
> —W.308; W-166.2:2-3

Passing Through

Our essential ineffectiveness in being able to perceive the Kingdom of Heaven occurs as we see ourselves living in time — laden with guilt from the past, fearful of the future, unaware of eternity.

Surprisingly, some of the best descriptions of eternity are found in the scientific study of matter. The descriptions of the subatomic world offered by modern physicists sound very like the descriptions of the mystics. Somewhere in the core of everything, they say, time stops. From this vantage point, a point outside time, one attains a transpersonal perspective. From this perspective it is not necessary to judge the world, nor find ourselves caught in its problems. We may act in the world, as surely as did Jesus, but we need not worry about the world.

What makes one person peaceful and happy, another sick and depressed? Somewhere, in the middle of it all, is the activity of God or the activity of ego. The activity of God is eternal. The activity of the ego is limited and destined to end in time.

An American tourist once paid a visit to a renowned Polish rabbi, Hofetz Chaim. He was astonished to see that the rabbi's home was merely a simple room, with only books, a table, a chair, and a cot.

> The tourist asked, "Rabbi, where is your furniture?"
> Hofetz Chaim replied, "Where is yours?"
> The puzzled American asked, "Mine? But I'm only a visitor here. I'm only passing through."
> The rabbi replied, "So am I."

Because Heaven transcends time, our only true and eternal identity is as an inhabitant of Heaven. We are only visiting here. We are all wayfarers, sojourners, seekers on the path to Heaven. We may go away to school, or to work, or take a vacation, but someday we will return home.

Heaven or Hell?

Insofar as we find this a confining place, we live in hell. Insofar as we find the unlimited here, we live in Heaven.

> *"The mind is its own place,*
> *and in itself*
> *Can make a heaven of hell,*
> *or a hell of heaven."*
> —John Milton, *Paradise Lost*

This place can be seen as hell. The world is full of war, sickness, depression, poverty, and powerlessness. We can get caught in the judgment and condemnation of this place, but it is more fun to reflect Heaven here.

There is no need to resist the inevitable. We are all children of God and we will inevitably inherit the Kingdom of Heaven. Jesus in the Gospels tells us that unless we become like little children we cannot enter the Kingdom of God

> *"'Except ye become as little children' means*
> *that unless you fully recognize*
> *your complete dependence on God,*
> *you cannot know the real power of the Son*
> *in his true relationship with the Father."*
> —T.10; T-1.V.3:4

Getting back to God, getting back to Heaven means recognizing our dependency on God and the guiltlessness that must be ours as His children. I once heard a preacher describe Heaven as a place of pearly gates and streets of gold. He was describing an idealized form of this world.

"Heaven is not a place nor a condition.
It is merely an awareness of perfect oneness
and the knowledge that there is nothing else,
nothing outside this oneness,
and nothing else within."
—T.359; T-18.VI.1:5-6

Heaven is but a matter of awareness — and that awareness is possible at any moment. At any moment we might realize: "The Kingdom of Heaven is within me," or better, "The Kingdom of Heaven *is* me."

We Already Live in the Kingdom

According to the *Course* the world will not end in a bang nor in a whimper. It will merely cease to be because its usefulness as a place of learning will have passed.

"The world will end in joy,
because it is a place of sorrow.
The world will end in peace,
because it is a place of war.
The world will end in laughter,
because it is a place of tears."
—M.36; M-14.5:1-5

"Have faith only in only this one thing,
and it will be sufficient:
God wills you be in Heaven,
and nothing can keep you from it,
or it from you.
Your wildest misperceptions,
your weird imaginings,
your blackest nightmares all mean nothing.
They will not prevail against the peace God wills for you."
—T.249; T-13.XI.7:1-3

Chapter 19

There Is No Enemy

Who Is the Devil?

On the way home from church one Sunday one young boy turned to another and said: "Do you believe there really is such a thing as the devil?"

To this the other replied, "Naw, it's just like Santa Claus. He's really your dad."

The word for "devil" in the Greek translation of the New Testament is *diabolos*, which means "slanderer." Paul and the Gospel writers call the devil "Satan," meaning the "adversary" or "accuser." According to ancient rabbinical teaching, Satan is responsible for the *yecer hara*, or the evil impulse in human beings. Who is the devil? Is the devil a person?

One of the reasons the *Course in Miracles* is so appealing is because the *Course* teaches peace. The foundation set up to publish the *Course* is called the Foundation for Inner Peace, in the realization that if there is to be peace, it must be something that begins inside. The *Course* teaches quite clearly:

> *"To have peace, teach peace to learn it."*
> —T.98; T-6.V.B.

According to the *Course* the devil is a projection of the ego, and the affirmation of the reality of the devil is an attempt to deny responsibility for our own guilt by projecting guilt onto an external agent. If you can project onto an external agent, then you can say that whatever trouble there is in the world is someone else's fault. If you can identify evil as "out there," then of course you can "justify" attacking or killing that agent.

*"The mind can make the belief in separation very real
and very fearful, and this belief is the devil."*
−T.45; T-3.VII.5:1

The devil is not someone out there who must be hated, despised, and fought against. The devil is not an individual person or a physical being. The devil is the belief in separation. Someone once said that God created human beings in His image and then human beings turned around and created God in their image.

*"Man has created the devil,
he has created him in his own image and likeness."*
−Fyodor M. Dostoyevski

God has created human beings in His likeness and image as Spirit. We have created the devil out of our own guilt and our own likeness as an ego, as a separator, as a body only.

Rev. Jimmy Swaggart said in his memorable tearful sermon of Sunday, February 21, 1988, that the devil had tempted him and he had given in to temptation. Headlines in the newspaper on February 22 read: "Swaggart Fights Devil — Devil Wins!"

Swaggart was an amazingly effective preacher. His strong use of emotions, of fear and tears, had a powerful effect that pulled deeply at the heartstrings of his audience. I watched him one Sunday evening when he was trying to make his comeback. He was speaking of the devil again. He said the devil was a mighty enemy.

Do you think of yourself as having an enemy? Who is your enemy? Whom do you fight against? Dr. Carl Jung has shown in his work on archetypes and symbols that whenever we give psychic energy to any concept we also give it power. The *Course* says that as we make something real we give it power over us. Thus, as we make the illusions of this world real we give them power over us. The more we make the devil real, the more power we give the devil.

The *Course* also says that every system of thought begins either with a making or a creating. God creates while we make. To free ourselves from our own guilt we have "made up" the idea of the devil as an external force because we do not want to look at the guilt we have buried inside.

The devil exists insofar as the ego exists. Insofar as the ego has nothing to do with God's Kingdom and eternity, the ego and the devil exist not at all. Because of the ego's strong need to project, it is easy to find an enemy. I remember listening to a Memorial Day speech in 1989 in which the speaker, a local chief of police, suggested that what our country needed was a "good war." He emphasized that we should not engage in an unpopular war like the Vietnam war. When he said we needed a "good war," everyone applauded. A year and a half later the Gulf war erupted and the "good war" came into existence. I'm reminded of Groucho Marx once saying that "military intelligence" was a contradiction in terms. How could there be any terms more contradictory than "good" and "war?"

Our Enemy — Ourselves

"A man has no enemy worse than himself."
—Cicero

"Every man is his own chief enemy."
—Anacharsis

"Yet is every man his greatest enemy,
and his own executioner."
—Thomas Browne

"You have no enemy except yourself."
—T.523; T-26.X.3:6

Insofar as I have ever had what looks like an enemy, I've been my own worst enemy. What's true for me is no doubt true for us all. No matter how much Swaggart may blame the devil, Swaggart has been his own worst enemy. No one was whispering in his ear. What is true for Swaggart is true for us all.

"Man's chief enemy is his own unruly nature
and the dark forces pent up within him."
—Ernest Jones

In the same way the *Course* would ask us to look at our selfish, separating ego self and then to ask the Holy Spirit to help us see beyond
it. We need to realize that the dark side is not in fact who we really
are. It's part of the illusion. It's part of what we made up. It isn't real
and we come to know that it is not real as we begin to discover our
real Self, which was not "made up" by us but "created" by God.

The task is not to condemn the shadow or try to extract, destroy,
or cut it from our being. The task is not to kill it. The more we try
to kill the devil the more we make real what we would destroy. The
task is to realize that the shadow side of our personality is not in truth
who we really are. There is nothing to be afraid of. We are in truth
"one Self united with our Creator," and that Self cannot even conceive
of murder.

Adlof Hitler, Joseph McCarthy, Jimmy Swaggart — all found some
enemy who they said had to be destroyed. For Hitler it was the Jews,
for McCarthy the communists, for Swaggart the devil.

> *"No one can doubt the ego's skill*
> *in building up false cases."*
> —T.145; T-8.VIII.8:4

In the February 1988 edition of *Christian Today* magazine there
was an article entitled, "When Christians Meet New Agers." The title
suggests that you cannot be a Christian and at the same time a part of
what is very broadly referred to as the New Age. The article goes so
far as to say that the New Age movement is "an antichrist system to
be resisted and refuted vigorously."

In my life's journey some of the most loving, openhearted, honest, and truthful people I have ever met might well be part of what is
considered the New Age. Many "New Agers" are real "Christians" in
the sense of bringing into practice what Jesus taught about love, non-
judgment, and our reality as spirit. *Christian Today*'s antichrist does
not exist any more than the devils of Salem or the devil who tempted
Swaggart.

There is no enemy.

Opposition to Your Truth

That there is in truth no enemy does not mean that we are not going to run into opposition in the world. There will be opposition, but opposition is not an enemy. When people oppose us on issues that are true to us, or we find people who believe differently from us, and think we should change our mind or lifestyle to their way of thinking, we may encounter what "looks like" an enemy. In this sense, our supposed enemy may also have a positive influence on us by enabling us to get to our own truth even more clearly.

"Our enemies are those who
strengthen our nerves and sharpen our skill."
—Edmund Burke

While Hitler, McCarthy, and Swaggart made up nonexistent enemies, Jesus, Martin Luther, Gandhi, and Martin Luther King, Jr., found it a challenge and a blessing to face people who strongly opposed them and did not look upon them as enemies. Jesus' greatest opposition came from the Saducees and the Pharisees. He never wanted it so. No one wants to be opposed. But he had to remain true to himself. His truth was frightening to the Pharisees and the Saducees, who were no doubt jealous of him. He was a threat to the power they had held so long. The "threat" came from his truth. He was true and they were scared. He was talking about a world God created. They were trying to defend a system of belief they made up for themselves.

Martin Luther faced incredible opposition from the church. He never wanted it so. He never wanted to leave the church. It was the church who excommunicated Luther, not Luther who extricated himself from the church. He was a very spiritual and intellectual man. After he was excommunicated, he had no choice but to go on his own. Because he remained true to himself and spoke the truth as he saw it, the Protestant Reformation was born. Yet he could say:

"My soul is too glad and too great
to be at heart the enemy of any man."

Gandhi's opposition was British imperialism. He too had to stand up for the truth of the right to be free. He too had to stand up for justice. Eventually the truth must prevail. Truth is the important thing; it is the way to peace. Because he stuck to the truth Gandhi's truth won out.

Martin Luther King, Jr., was opposed by the racists. He would not have it so. In several of his speeches he said how much he wished that the opposition he found around him did not exist. Eventually the truth of love proved stronger than racism and many civil rights reforms were born because of this wonderful man.

When I first entered the ministry I was very committed and ready to get to work — to get to the truth, to find what it was that was going on at a deeper level. I kept saying "What does it all mean — this life? What is it all about?" Throughout college, seminary, and graduate school I became fascinated with the pursuit of truth as it was revealed in many different expressions, in many cultures and religions.

> *"To study different religions*
> *need not imply infidelity to one's own faith,*
> *but rather it may be enlarged by seeing how other people*
> *have sought for reality and have been enriched by their search."*
> —Geoffrey Parrinder

I discovered that truth was not the sole property of the Christians. Indeed, it became clear to me that all the world's great teachings are the same. Perceived differences are just that: *perceived* differences developed by the followers of different traditions, not by the founders themselves. The more I said this the more I found myself in opposition to the church. With immense naïveté, I kept thinking that other clergy would become interested in the truth as expressed in the *Course* or in Buddhism or in Taoism or in any of the thousands of paths to God that exist. But that is not what happened. Finally, the day came when I had to leave. I wanted to be an "intra-preneuer" working within the church, but it wasn't to be.

Now I realize how important it was that this happen — how strong it has made me, how clear the greater truth. Now I can speak without guarding my words and can as easily quote Buddha as Jesus of the Gospels or *A Course in Miracles*. The truth is we are all people here. The truth is there are many ways to God. The truth is: *There is no enemy.*

It is wonderful to know that there are no enemies, not even the church. If I have ever have had an enemy, it has been my own shadowy self distracted by lesser things while greater vision was possible. I now know that you can't change structures until you change yourself. There are people who disagree with me and with whom, it may be said, I disagree. But it is helpful to remember that disagreement is simply disagreement.

There is no enemy.

Our task is to keep on growing — to keep being ourselves at our very best, to realize the Kingdom of God, and to help others see it as well. If we can get past our own misperceptions, then we all can see: *There is no devil and there is no enemy.*

Chapter 20

There Is No Hell

"The Holy Spirit teaches thus: There is no hell."
—T.281; T-15.I.7:1

I taught public speaking for many years. There's a section in the *Public Speaking* textbook on the use of emotion as a means of motivation. The book suggests six forms of motivational appeal, three of which appeal to negative emotions and three to the positive. The positive appeals are to pride, respect, and reverence. The negative motivators are shame, fear, and anger. The *Course* says of itself that its primary motivational appeal is the attainment of peace (T.464; T-24.Intro.1.1). The purpose of the *Course* is to remove the blocks to an awareness of love's presence. It's not here to frighten us. It's here to bring us peace.

It's an interesting psychology that suggests that it is good to frighten people. Such approaches may temporarily provide the desired result, but you have to wonder whether you've really changed anyone for the better. There was an interesting attempt at this a few years ago in a program called Scared Straight, which was initiated by the New Jersey prison system. Young delinquents were taken into prison and told by hardened convicts what would happen to them if they came to prison. Although the program claimed positive results, a follow-up study showed the program actually backfired. Those youngsters who participated in the program committed more crimes after the Scared Straight program than a control group from the same neighborhoods who did not participate in the program.

What Is Hell?

The concept of hell does not exist at the foundation of all religions. There is no hell as such in Judaism or in Christian Science. As with *A Course in Miracles,* Mary Baker Eddy taught that evil and sin, in league with error, sickness, and death, are products of false perception and do not exist in the all-knowing, all-loving Mind of God.

According to the *Course,* hell is the ego's illusory picture of a world beyond death that would punish us for our sins. The dictionary definition of hell says: "In Christianity the place where sinners and unbelievers go after death for torment and eternal punishment."

Hell is a not very nice idea; it is perpetuated by those who would seek out sin as testimony to its reality. I have a *Christian Ministers' Manual of Illustrations* for use with sermons. I looked up the illustrations it has to offer about hell. They all talked about unspeakable horror, utter terror, fire, brimstone, wailing and the gnashing of teeth. One toothless old man, who had heard his preacher talking about the gnashing of teeth, asked what would happen to him if he went to hell, as he had no teeth. His minister replied: "Teeth will be provided."

The essential difference between the *Course* and traditional Christianity is that the *Course* is a monistic system while traditional Christianity is a dualistic system. In this sense the *Course* is closer to the Vedanta of Hinduism or to Buddhism than it is to Christianity.

If you posit the existence of two forces — one of good and one of evil — that are constantly in "battle" with each other, and the battle never won, then you have Heaven and hell, God and the devil. But if there is only God, only Heaven, only Love, only the Eternal, then you cannot have hell. As this world is a world of oppositions, it is easy for us to believe in Heaven and hell. The ego thus reasons that:

> *"If Heaven exists, there must be hell as well,*
> *for contradiction is the way we make what we perceive,*
> *and what we think is real."*
> —W.257; W-138.1:3

Once the conscious choice for Heaven has been made then you see that what is whole can have no opposite. From this standpoint, only Heaven is.

In this world it is possible to experience hellish states. Heaven by definition is an experience of freedom. Hell can be thought of as the loss of freedom, a state in which we have no power or control over our environment or its effect upon us. In this sense hell existed in slave ships, in war, in the concentration camps. But all of these states, as horrible as they were, were not eternal and were escaped by bodily death, if nothing else.

I entitled the written description of my death experience "Holy Hell." It was holy because of what I saw as possibilities for consciousness through it, a world thousands of times greater than this one. It was hell because I did not want to die and the experience can be understood essentially as my ego's encounter with death. I was sure I had died and could not bear the thought of no longer existing in a particularized body in space and time. I did not know how to control what seemed to be happening to me, and for that reason it was hellish.

Fear Is Hell

The *Course* describes fear as hell (T.617; T-31.VIII.7:6). Fear is always of something in the future. As the *Course* expresses it:

> *"The belief in hell is inescapable*
> *to those who identify with the ego.*
> *Their nightmares and their fears are all associated with it.*
> *The ego teaches that hell is in the future,*
> *for this is what all its teaching is directed to.*
> *Hell is its goal."*
> —T.280; T-15.I.4:1-4

It's not what is happening now that frightens us. It is what might happen. Even in an emergency situation, such as an automobile accident, when conscious awareness is heightened our fears are still of the future.

> *"The only way in which the ego allows the fear of hell*
> *to be experienced is to bring hell here,*
> *but always as a foretaste of the future."*
> —T.281; T-15.I.6:6

Even traditional Christianity describes hell as separation and the feeling that it is impossible to reach back to God. Hell is created in our special relationships, in our lack of willingness to forgive, in our inability to let things be. Hell arises in our anger, our self-righteousness, and our arrogance in thinking that people who do not think as we do are condemned to hell.

Jesus and the Devil

When we read of Jesus' temptation in the desert, we can understand the event as Jesus' encounter with his own ego — the temptation to give in to the ego and seek worldly power and goods rather than listen to the Voice for God. The good news of the temptation story is that Jesus never gave in to the ego (devil) but resisted the temptation. Unlike you and me, he never got caught in the machinations and fears of the ego. He recognized his true identity and held to it. Salvation for any of us comes as we do what he did, as we too become aware of our true identity, recognize our eternal home as Heaven, and accept our part in the Atonement. The *Course* says:

> *"You can reflect Heaven here."*
> —T.271; T-14.IX.5:2

If we can reflect Heaven here, let's get on with reflecting Heaven rather than engaging in witch hunting and its inevitable outcome, condemnation of our brothers and sisters. Is it not more fun to be offering peace through our forgiveness rather than seeking out sin and engaging in further separation?

It is an interesting theology that claims that we come into the world one time, we get one chance to get our perceptions and behavior right, and we are then either condemned forever to the eternal fires of hell or rewarded with eternal bliss. How could a God of Love create such a horrible idea as an eternal hell for one of His children who was ignorant of His will? No earthly parents would conceive of such treatment for their child. How could God, who is far more perfect in His Love, do so?

A similar problem arises in a theology that posits a belief in original sin and suggests that we are condemned and that our only hope is the grace of Jesus. Father Matthew Fox's notion of "original blessing" has shaken this idea more than a little. According to the *Course* our original true identity is that of a child of God, not of the devil.

There is a movement sweeping Christian churches today called millennialism. As we approach the year 2000, more and more preachers are turning to the book of Revelation, where we read of a conspiracy of evil against God and His rule, and of Satan's influence. The New Testament is steeped in a dualistic view of human nature and abounds with descriptions of a cosmic struggle between the forces of good and evil. Nineteen of the twenty-seven books of the New Testament are concerned about the devil and forces of evil. As a point of interest, the word "God" appears 3,616 times in the *Course* and the word "devil" appears 8 times.

Hell is the experience of being separated from God — of not being able to participate in His Kingdom. *Hell exists insofar as the ego exists* and keeps itself in hell because of its fear of Heaven. But *hell does not exist because the ego does not exist.* It is all part of a bad dream, a nightmare. Though we may believe that it is possible to be separated from the Love of God, ultimately we cannot be separate. We must eventually return to the Source from which we came. No matter how far we wander, we must eventually return Home and give up the idea of condemnation and separation.

Jesus' favorite picture of God in the New Testament is that of a Father. He refers to God as Abba — literally, "Daddy." He says, *"I and the Father are one."* He begins the Lord's Prayer with *"Our Father who art in Heaven."* Parables like the prodigal son clearly picture God as an all-loving Father who created us and loves us all equally. The story of the lost sheep suggests that there is no one who is exempt from God's love. As a loving Father, He is not about to reject us or condemn us to hell because we are ignorant of His will.

Chapter 21

There Is No Time

Jesus tells his disciples many things. He also tells them that there are many things that he cannot tell them because they are not yet ready to hear. I wonder if one of the things the disciples were not yet ready to hear, because they could not understand it, was his explanation of time and eternity.

Nineteen hundred years after Jesus, there lived another man who, though not a religious prophet, because of his incredible insights into the workings of nature was certainly a prophet. Though not a saint, he was without doubt a genius. His name was Albert Einstein.

Two thousand years ago, the disciples could not yet understand Jesus' explanation of time. Nearly two thousand years passed before someone could explain it. Now, many years after Einstein, few people understand it. Few people understand it because it requires a leap in the imagination. The mind must make an intuitive jump. We must try to see things in a wholly new way.

Time is Relative

Einstein discovered that time is relative. It can slow down. It can speed up. It can stop. Einstein's secretary once asked him to explain to her the theory of relativity and he replied:

> *"Two hours with a beautiful woman seems like two minutes.*
> *Two minutes on a hot stove seems like two hours.*
> *That is relativity!"*

We've all heard it said that if someone were to leave earth, travel to another galaxy, and then somehow return, his childhood friends would be old men and women while our space traveler would have aged very little. We accept this because the scientists tell us it is true, but why it is true?

Kenneth Wapnick, *The Vast Illusion: Time in A Course in Miracles;* Stephen Hawking, *A Brief History of Time;* Stanislof Grof, *Realms of the Human Unconscious;* Fritjof Capra, *The Tao of Physics;* and Gary Zukav, *The Dancing Wu Li Masters* all give us a new insight into time and eternity and a whole field of study coming to be known as new physics.

The *Course* draws a distinction between linear time, or history, and eternity, the realm of God's Kingdom. The dictionary defines "eternity" as "timelessness." God lives in *timelessness.* Christ is *timeless.* You, the You that you really are, are *timeless.* Jesus stepped away from eternity and came into time, but he never forgot eternity. From the standpoint of the *Course,* when we come into this world we too step away from eternity. Unlike Jesus we get caught in time and lose sight of eternity.

Think of it this way: the center of a cyclone is a point of absolute stillness. Around the outside of the cyclone there is an immense amount of chaos, but in the center everything stops. It is possible to step into the center where chaos has stopped and only eternity is. In fact, though you may not remember it, everyone has had the experience of stepping away from time. From this vantage point, you may see chaos whirling around you. To step out of the center and back into the world is to step back into activity, movement, time, and chaos.

Imagine that you can step back in at any point, in any society or in any body. If you step into the world as a Hindu you will see the world through Hindu eyes. If you step in as a woman, you have a perspective different from that of a man. If you step back into the twentieth century, you see it differently from how you would see it if you stepped back into the seventeenth century or the twenty-second century.

Watch the Nickelodeon channel on TV where all the sitcoms and ads are from the 1950s and you may think that people of that time were living with a strange and somewhat primitive interpretation of reality. Well, it's only forty years later. What would it be like to jump, say, to the year 3000 and look back at the 1990s? Will our present interpretation of reality not seem pretty silly? If it's true then, it's true now. When you look back at your own past you may think you did some things that were pretty silly. Fortunately, you say now you know better.

I See Only The Past

Exercise No. 7 from *A Course in Miracles* says: *"I see only the past."* While the exercise says of itself that it may be difficult to believe, it is the rationale for all the exercises that follow it.

Exercise No. 8 says, *"My mind is preoccupied with past thoughts."*

Exercise No. 9 says, *"I see nothing as it is now."*

We are always living in the past. We are perpetually rehearsing the past. All of our guilt is based on the past; without our past we would have no guilt.

Our egos are innately caught in time — in a story, in a particular moment in history, in a specific location. We talk about the past, are hung up about who we were in the past, have guilty feelings about the past. We worry and project the past into the future, missing the present.

The *Course* says that "now" is as close as we can get to eternity. But we keep missing now because we keep falling back into time or projecting ourselves forward in time.

> *To another He said, "Follow me." But he said, "Lord, let me first go and bury my father."*
>
> *But He said to him, "Leave the dead to bury their own dead; but as for you, go and proclaim the kingdom of God."*
> —Luke 9:59–60

The past is past. Now is now. This moment, were we really awake to it, would be so incredible we would not have time to worry over the past nor to project the future.

Aldous Huxley, bending over the body of his dying wife, Maria, whispered into her ear:

> *"Let go; let go.*
> *Forget the body; leave it lying here;*

it is of no importance now.
Go forward into the light.
Let yourself be carried into the light.
No memories, no regrets, no looking backward,
no apprehensive thoughts about your own or anyone else's future."
—Jon Mundy, *Learning to Die*, p. 69

Dropping Personal History

To be born anew we have to let go of the old stuff we've been carrying with us.

"To be born again is to let the past go,
and look without condemnation upon the present."
—T.234; T-13.VI.3:5

Don Juan of the Castañeda series says we gain the moment only as we drop personal history.

"One day, I discovered I didn't need personal history,
so, like drinking, I dropped it."
—Carlos Castañeda,
Tales of Power, p. 20

Having a personal history keeps us from now, so it also keeps us from eternity. If we could erase personal history, says Don Juan, it would make us free from the encumbering thoughts of others. Don Juan pointed out that Carlos didn't know anything about him beyond what he himself had told him. He could be someone else for all Carlos knew. Carlos, on the other hand, renewed his personal history daily by telling his relatives and friends everything he did. If you have no personal history, no explanations are needed.

According to Don Juan, when people know our personal history, know exactly who we are, what we believe and what we stand for, they have a certain amount of control over us. They expect us to behave in a certain way, and if we don't, they become surprised and/or disillusioned. To express it simply: "If you don't have a story, you don't have to fit it."

Many of us get frustrated in this world because life in time has to fit into a box that pins us down as a specific kind of person with specific kinds of professions (teacher, minister, secretary, doctor, etc.) with specific pasts (college, graduate school, professional organizations). The more our position is defined, the harder it is to know truth and freedom. It may thus be easier for an unknown farmer going about his daily chores to be more blissfully alive, trusting, free and aware of his identity as a son of God than it is for a Hollywood star, trapped in the process of maintaining an image.

Dropping personal history — learning to die, stopping the world, stepping outside of time — gives us the opportunity to discover eternity. God lives in eternity.

I once asked a young man whom I knew had had a number of mystical experiences how far he had gone. He answered, "Where?" My question implied that there was a height to which he could ascend or a depth or width of consciousness that he might attain. These are spatial, temporal limitations. Space and time are ego perspectives. The mystical state is timeless.

> *"On this side of the bridge to timelessness*
> *you understand nothing.*
> *But as you step lightly across it, upheld by timelessness,*
> *you are directed straight to the Heart of God.*
> *At its center, and only there, you are safe forever,*
> *because you are complete forever."*
> —T.317; T-16.IV.13:6

The Ego Lives in Time

Timelessness is our only reality.

> *"God and the soul are not in space-time,*
> *but belong to the realms that are intrinsically or essentially real.*
> *Time ends where there is no before or after.*
> *We perceive only a shadow of the real,*
> *living in a world created and sustained by our own cognition."*
> —Meister Eckhart

> *"It is believed by most that time passes;*
> *in actual fact, it stays where it is.*

This idea of passing may be called time,
but it is an incorrect idea,
for since one sees it only as passing,
one cannot understand that it stays just where it is."
—Zen Master Dogen

When we don't have to live in time, when we don't have to live up to an image or be caught up in our own personal drama, we can have an awareness of eternity. It is possible to be so in the moment that past and future lose their significance. We may become aware of this at death. But we don't have to wait for death and the dissolution of our bodies to find the truth.

When we lose our body, our most immediate form of identity within space and time, we are forced to look to a greater reality. When the body is not perceived as our primary reality, its past and its projected future disappear.

Then, only God is.

Then, only purity exists.

Then, only the moment exists.

To know this is to be incredibly wealthy.

Guilt and Peace Cannot Coexist

Throughout the whole of his life Jesus never forgot that God was his Father. He knew that he was God's Son and that Heaven was his home. Coming home in this sense means stepping out of the trap of time. We too could see what Jesus saw. We could live so fully in the present that past and future would fail to imprison us. The past would not be a cause of guilt nor the future a place of fear. The world of sin, guilt, and fear have nothing to do with God and His Kingdom. Sin, guilt, and fear are of our own making. They are what keep us locked in time. There is no guilt or fear in Heaven. Were any of us in the center of time as Jesus was, we also would have no guilt or fear.

Jesus stepped from eternity into time to tell us about eternity. Eternity is a perfectly peaceful place. It is our eternal home. My encounter with death led me to believe that we always have been and will be. I'm not suggesting reincarnation. Reincarnation, after all, is a time-bound concept. I'm just saying, *Always must be now.*

> *"There is no road to travel on*
> *and no time to travel through."*
> —T.222; T-13.I.7:3

The Holy Instant

The *Course* says that at any moment we can choose to have a holy instant of forgiveness and peace. In the holy instant we transcend our limited view of ourselves and others, let go of our individual soap operas, drop our personal histories, and step out of time. The only thing that can die in time is that which is mortal. The body may be buried in the earth but the body is finite. The soul is eternal.

You already are.

You are eternal.

You always have been. You always will be.

We need not be caught in time. Our real home is eternal. We can live with an awareness of eternity. Jesus stepped away from the center and came into this world. Unlike you and me, he never forgot the center. He never got caught in the projection of guilt. Though drama developed around him, he never got caught up in the drama. His awareness of his Father remained alive inside him.

He was able, by parable and analogies, to tell us something of eternity. He understood that there was nothing to defend and went to the cross to show us that there is no reality to death.

There is nothing that has to be achieved. Jesus tells us that whatever is real and valuable is already within. It is more a matter of "realization" or "remembering" than doing something about our ego's goals. The Sonship is not out there. The Kingdom of Heaven is not something we shall find in the future. Eternity is available right now and our task is to delight in the present.

From four thousand years ago comes this advice given by a maiden to the Babylonian hero Gilgemish in his search for the meaning of life:

> *"Gilgemish, wither hurriest thou?*
> *The life that thou seekest thou will not find.*
> *O Gilgemish, let thy belly be filled.*
> *Daily celebrate a feast,*
> *Day and night dance and make merry.*
> *Look joyfully on the child that grasps thy hand,*
> *Be happy with the wife in thine arms!"*

We can be happy this moment. Not for a single moment do we need to delay. There is nothing we have to hold on to. All that is needed is available this moment. We just have to open our eyes.

Forgive where we need to forgive. Speak the truth where it needs to be spoken. Love a little more and we can be free. We don't have to become God. We don't have to rush to achieve something. The Sonship already is. We just have to see it.

> *"You are but asked to let the future go,*
> *and place it in God's Hands.*
> *And you will see by your experience*
> *that you have laid the past and present*
> *in His Hands as well,*
> *because the past will punish you no more,*
> *and future dread will now be meaningless."*
> —W.360; W-pI.194.4:5-6

Part IV

Nothing Real
Can Be Threatened

Chapter 22

There Is No Love but God's

The Law of Love

When the *Course* talks about the law of love, all it means is the principle of giving and receiving. It just means that as we give out love so must we inevitably experience love coming back our way. It is a principle, a description of the way things work: just as when we attack so do we experience attack coming back our way.

> *"For if Love is sharing,*
> *how can you find it except through itself?*
> *Offer it and it will come to you,*
> *because it is drawn to itself.*
> *But offer attack and love will remain hidden,*
> *for it can live only in peace."*
> —T.217; T-12.VIII.1:5

Love is a law that goes beyond all laws. It just is, in perfect purity and peace.

There is no love but God's; God is the total, the Tao. The first commandment is to love God. The second is like it. How are we going to love God? How can we love something we cannot see? A bridge is needed; hence, the second commandment. The easiest way to love God is to love those about us. The easiest way to love those about us is not to judge them.

There are not different kinds of love. The *Course* says love has no separate parts and no degrees (W.225; W-pI.127.1:4). We cannot love sometimes and hate at other times. We cannot love some people and withhold our love from others. Love must be total, complete. As we love each other, love starts expanding outwardly like concentric circles created by a stone dropped in a pond. It touches everyone. When you have the feeling of love coming from your heart, you know it goes outward to everyone.

If you would love God and know His love for you, love those who are the closest to you in time and space. Start by loving the familiar and let love expand: love animals, trees, and rocks. Diane is always telling our animals that she loves them. "I love you Rudi, I love you Cindy, I love you Skunk, I love you Pepper, I love you Mussy."

All Humanity Is Us

Our neighbor is nothing other than our own self, our own being in another form, a different shape. Someone else is brown or black or white. Colors and sizes just reflect differences in the terrain. The soul is colorless. In Hindustani the word "disciple" means someone who is colorless. We are not the body, nor are we the mind nor even the heart. Our bodies are different because they have come through different terrains of biology and heredity. Our minds have been conditioned with different philosophies, religious traditions, and moral perspectives.

Differences exist only on the surface. There is a deep inner part of our mind that is forever connected with God. No matter how deeply we may have buried that memory, it is there and can be recalled when we start loving. As souls we are colorless. There is no difference and we are all one. Soul is the only thing that is eternal. It is the only thing that is truly of God.

Diane tells the story of a friend whose father was a rough, difficult man — a "lawyer," not a "lover." The son had a lot of trouble dealing with his father and often felt hatred for him. Then one day the father, who was now getting older, was hit by a car while crossing the street. A few days later he suffered a stroke. He never quite recovered. After that his mind changed, and he became more childlike, more loving. Now the man whom the son had hated was altogether different and dependent upon his son to care for him. What a dilemma. The old man whom the son had hated was no longer hateful. Now he was loving. As the son was willing to let go of the past, a real healing occurred in him and in the relationship. All that was left, all that was real between them was love.

It's always like that: buried within, sometimes not even too deeply, is the love of God trying to get out. But our egos have got it all covered over; something is needed to release the love.

> *"Because of your Father's Love you can never forget Him,*
> *for no one can forget what God Himself place in his memory.*
> *You can deny it, but you cannot lose it."*
> —T.218; T-12.VIII.4:1

Jesus suggests that when it comes to loving we should try going the second mile. Going the second mile is an addition to the idea of doing good for others. Jesus asks us to love others as ourselves. We can't truly love others when we don't love ourselves. If you can't go the second mile for yourself, how can you go the second mile for another? Sometimes in order to lose weight or drop some addiction or negative behavior pattern we have to go the second mile. It requires a little willingness, but just a little. By going the second mile we do something extra. I like the definition of success given by Don Juan of the Carlos Castañeda series:

> *"Success must come gently, with a great deal of effort*
> *but with no stress or obsession."*

What does it mean to do something with effort but with no stress or obsession? When we do something extra for ourselves, like exercising to keep in shape, we give a little extra effort. We find ourselves loving ourselves. Going the second mile with someone else means:

- being patient even when our patience is tried;

- not getting angry when we might have gotten angry before;

- not being hurt even when we have "seemingly?" been betrayed.

By going the second mile we discover more about loving — ourselves and others. Going the second mile makes it easier for God to help us along the way.

You Are as Close to God as You Can Get

Jesus says *"Love your neighbor as yourself."* We cannot love others without loving ourselves and we cannot love ourselves without loving God, because there is no love but God's. Heaven is inside us; therefore God is inside us — not inside our bodies, which are not eternal, but inside the mind, which is eternal and is connected with the eternal mind of God. If we accept ourselves, if we love ourselves, everything else becomes automatic — including the love of God. We cannot hate ourselves and love others. God has loved us so much that He has made a temple in us. He lives within us. The Kingdom of Heaven is where God lives. If we reject ourselves we reject our nearness to God.

There is an old Danish story of a spider who lived high in the rafters of an old barn. One day the spider lowered himself to a beam where he found the flies more prolific and more easily caught. He therefore decided to live permanently on this lower level. He spun for himself a comfortable web. One day he noticed the line down which he had come and said to himself that he no longer needed it. So he snapped it and destroyed the support for his whole web.

A thread joins us with the ultimate. We have come from God and we are going to Him. Everything eventually goes back to its source. Sometimes we might feel like the spider. We come into this world and look up at that thread and think, "That thing is in the way." We snap the line and then we go mad.

Insofar as we are mad, insofar as we are caught in anger and judgment and fear, we are removed from God. Those who are very angry, who are very self-righteous, are very far removed. Yet anyone of us can be brought back in an instant. Sometimes something has to happen to remind us who we really are. The death of a loved one might do it. Our own encounter with death might do it. It might happen more simply: just by meditating and praying and opening our hearts to love others, we might once again remember.

Love is our river of life, our eternal source of recreating ourselves. Jesus is like a honeybee that finds a field filled with flowers. She comes back and dances a dance of for her friends to tell them she has found sunshine and flowers. "Come," she says, "follow me." Jesus is like the honeybee who found the elixir of life, the entrance to the Kingdom of Heaven. He comes and he dances a dance and says *"Come, follow me."*

Chapter 23

The Happy Dream

Despite this world of illusion there is hope. The *Course* describes a kind of dreaming called the happy dream, which God gives us to replace our fearful dreams. Not all dreams have to be nightmares or expressions of anxiety. In the happy dream we begin to dream of others' kindness instead of their mistakes; we dream of healing instead of hurting, pleasure instead of pain. In happy dreams there is no terror and no death. The happy dream prepares us for release and freedom.

> *"Happy dreams come true,*
> *not because they are dreams,*
> *but only because they are happy.*
> *And so they must be loving.*
> *Their message is 'Thy Will be done.'*
> *and not, 'I want it otherwise.'"*
> —T.357; T-18.V.4:1-3

The happy dream is the Holy Spirit's correction for the ego's misperception and its dream of pain and suffering. The happy dream is still part of the illusion (after all, it is a dream), yet it is a dream that can lead us beyond illusion. Though still illusory it is no longer fearful; because there is no fear in it, it can point beyond illusion. It is the dream of truth, love, and freedom.

Ultimately, the *Course* asks us to lay all dreaming aside and to awaken fully into a knowledge of God's presence in our lives. The choice is not between which dreams to keep, but only whether we want to continue to live in dreams or awaken from them. The dreams

we think we would like to keep can hold us back as much as those in
which fear is seen (T.569; T-29.IV.2:1).

How to Perpetuate Dreaming

To awaken we must first realize that we have been sleeping, that
we have been living in a world of foolish fantasy and fear. It is not
difficult to change a dream once the dreamer has been recognized. But
first we must become aware of the dreamlike nature of our lives.

One good way to stay asleep is to deny that we are sleeping or to
pretend we are perfectly awake. On an ego level we don't want to look
at guilt so we push it out of our awareness and thus render it inaccessible to correction. Denial, according to the *Course*, is the ego's belief
that it (the ego) is our father and not God. There are lots of mind
tricks we can use to keep our reality as a child of God out of our
awareness.

Freud's great contribution was the discovery of the power of repression, projection, and the immensity of the unconscious. Classical
ego defense mechanisms such as repression, regression, displacement,
reaction formation, and sublimation are stronger than we think. It is
easy to go about in a kind of numb, unconscious, and insensitive form
of sleepwalking, never really letting God's awareness get through. It
is easy to live within the world of the TV tube, books, movies, magazines, newspapers, tabloids, and our own fantasies to such an extent
that we cut ourselves off altogether from any form of awareness of
our true nature.

"Dreams of any kind are strange and alien to the truth."
—W.370; W-198.8:2

The Proper Form of Denial

What we need is a proper form of denial, and that is the denial
of error or the denial of illusion. It is the denial of the reality of the
illusion and fearful dream.

> *"The acceptance of peace is the denial of illusion,*
> *and sickness is an illusion.*
> *Yet every Son of God has the power to deny illusions*
> *anywhere in the Kingdom,*
> *merely by denying them completely in himself."*
> —T.172; T-10.III.7:2-3

We perpetuate dreaming by living in a world of gossip, jealousy, intrigue, suspicion, hiding, and manipulation. All forms of intrigue and hiding keep us asleep. The *Course* asks us not to give reality to someone else's personal drama and not to give reality to our own. It asks us to concentrate not on that which divides but rather on that which unites.

> *"Accepting the Atonement for yourself*
> *means not to give support to someone's dream*
> *of sickness and of death.*
> *It means that you share not his wish to separate,*
> *and let him turn illusions on himself.*
> *Nor do you wish that they be turned, instead, on you."*
> —T.555; T-28.IV.1-3

Through forgiveness and truth-speaking it is possible to lay all such deceptiveness aside. And we do in our heart of hearts want to lay it aside.

> *"If you but knew the glorious goal that lies beyond forgiveness,*
> *you would not keep hold on any thought,*
> *however light the touch of evil on it may appear to be."*
> —T.571; T-29.V.6:1

We can awaken to the perception of our brother and sister as sinless as ourselves. This is what forgiveness is. Love holds no grievances. And forgiveness is the end of dreams, because it is a dream of waking.

> *"Forgiving dreams are kind to everyone who figures in the dream.*
> *And so they bring the dreamer full release from dreams of fear."*
> —T.579; T.29.IX.10:3-4

We perpetuate dreaming by finding ways to sedate the body and keep ourselves asleep.

> *"You can indeed be 'drugged' by sleep,*
> *if you have misused it on behalf of sickness."*
> —T.147; T-8.IX.4:6

All attempts to fill our lives with idols continually leave us feeling empty and separated. The only solution for such dreaming is awakening. The peace we seek will never be found through further dreaming but arises only as we change our minds. We do not need to continually knock ourselves out with the variety of sedatives this world would offer.

The Dream of the Spirit

Once we admit that we have been dreaming the task is then to trust in the Holy Spirit — and allow His gentle dream to take the place of our fearful ones.

> *"Yet the Holy Spirit, too, has use for sleep,*
> *and can use dreams on behalf of waking if you let Him.*
> *How you wake is the sign of how you have used sleep.*
> *To whom did you give it?*
> *Under which teacher did you place it?*
> *Whenever you wake dispiritedly,*
> *it was not given to the Holy Spirit.*
> *Only when you awaken joyously*
> *have you utilized sleep according to His purpose."*
> —T.147; T-8.IX.3:8 and 4:1-5

The *Course* would ask us to come to true vision, to see things through the eyes of Christ, to look upon the world without condemnation. Vision is the means by which the Holy Spirit translates our nightmares into happy dreams. Awakening from the dream, we go ahead and love even when defensiveness seems easier, when it is perhaps not clear why we should love.

The happy dream is a dream of forgiveness in which the real world is seen and salvation attained. In the happy dream we relinquish all that we fear, bless those who persecute us, and turn our lives over to God in trust. In the happy dream, the way out of the tunnel and the road to clear perception become possible.

Think about some time in your own life when you have been truly joyous. What brought about that joy? Was it not because you found some new insight, some new opportunity, some new freedom, some development or awareness that became possible that was not there before? Perhaps you fell in love. In any event, you found yourself more in touch with who you were or wanted to be.

The happy dream is one in which our most heartfelt wishes, those that reflect our real nature as God's sons and daughters, are fulfilled. Happy dreams are those in which Heaven is reflected.

In the happy dream we find that we can have life on our own terms, which are the same terms as God's. When others are in agreement about our terms and we are in agreement with them, everything goes smoothly. The exciting news is that things of this world are transformed as we become increasingly aware of the Kingdom of Heaven.

Life does not have to be a win-lose proposition. It can be win-win. In win-win everybody experiences abundance. Everybody gets to wake up. Good, honest, cooperative business works this way. I give you business; you give me business. We both win. There are no losers in Heaven. There are no losers in honest business. We can experience Heaven right now by being committed to helping others experience the abundance of God's Kingdom.

The happy dream is a correction of misperception. In the happy dream we acknowledge the power of decision-making and recognize that with God we are in charge of our thoughts. Jesus says, *"As a man thinketh so is he."* So what would you like to think?

It is not God's will that we lie.

It is not God's will that we are defensive and angry.

It is not God's will that we are jealous or pessimistic.

We are in charge of our own thoughts, and we can think and do whatever we want. We can get caught in our ego and the dream of this world. We can feel hurt, angry, rejected. We can also gain a higher perspective and see above it all. It just requires what the *Course* calls *"a little willingness."* We can, at this moment, love whomever we are looking at — if we want to.

In the happy dream we grow and expand spiritually as we find God taking care of us. God is a good partner, a good boss. Ask the Holy Spirit what you should be doing with your life. The Holy Spirit will tell you. Remember, the Holy Spirit's voice is as loud as our willingness to listen.

In the happy dream we fulfill a unique destiny. Yet when we fulfill our unique destiny, we do something good for all humanity. As other people appreciate our happy dream and dream it along with us we all succeed.

Meaning — Purpose — Salvation

When we dream a happy dream meaning and purpose are automatic. Your life has a meaning and purpose. You can know what it is. In fact you already know — if you are willing to look at it. Ultimately we are concerned only with enlightenment, only with the completion of the Atonement, or salvation. Salvation is our only goal. Every goal outside of salvation is a misperception. That is not to condemn other goals — just to recognize that ultimately they don't satisfy us.

The Game that Happy Children Play

Though we may get caught in the games of this world it is possible to give them up.

"Salvation can be thought of as a game that happy children play.

It was designed by One Who loves His children,
and Who would replace their fearful toys with joyous games,
which teach them that the game of fear is gone.
His game instructs in happiness because there is no loser.

Everyone who plays must win,
and in his winning is the gain to everyone ensured.
The game of fear is gladly laid aside,
when children come to see the benefits salvation brings.

You who have played that you are lost to hope,
abandoned by your Father, left alone in terror in a fearful world
made mad by sin and guilt; be happy now.

Now a quiet time has come,
in which we put away the toys of guilt,
and lock out quaint and childish thoughts of sin
forever from the pure and holy minds of Heaven's children
and the Son of God."
—W.278-79; W-153.2:1-5,
13:1-3

When we are truly awake there is no pain, no difficulty, no problem. It means an awareness of one's true identity as an eternal being.
It means awareness that we are one with God, that the Atonement is
complete and there is nothing to be afraid of.

However black the world the light is in you.

Whenever we become afraid we take a step backward.

It is possible at any moment, at any holy instant to awaken again.

"You have not lost your innocence.
It is for this you yearn.
This is your heart's desire.
This is the voice you hear,
and this the call which cannot be denied.
The holy Child remains within you.
His home is yours.
Today He gives you His defenselessness,
and you accept it in exchange
for all the toys of battle you have made.
And now the way is open,
and the journey has an end in sight at last.
Be still an instant and go home with Him,
and be at peace a while."
—W.333; W-182.12:1-9

Remember:

"Rest does not come comes from sleeping
but from waking."
—T.71; T-5.II.10:4

Chapter 24

Fulfilling Personal Destiny

"The Kingdom of Heaven is like treasure hidden in a field that a man found and covered up; then in his joy, he sells all that he has and buys that field.

"Again, the Kingdom of Heaven is like a merchant in search of fine pearls, and, on finding one pearl of great value, went and sold all that he had and bought it."

—Matthew 13:44–46

What Is Our Function?

The famous Danish philosopher Søren Kierkegaard, engaged to the lovely Regina Olsen, about to move from his life of solitude to marriage, suddenly broke off the engagement. As much as he loved the beautiful Regina, he had come to the conclusion that marriage and his meditative life as a philosopher were incompatible.

Philosopher David Hume's father offered him a place in his growing business, which, if Hume had accepted it, would have meant a great fortune for the young Hume. Instead, Hume turned down his father's offer and chose the life of philosophic contemplation because, as he said, he had "an insatiable thirst for nothing but the pursuit of knowledge."

Jesus went to the cross; Kierkegaard canceled his marriage; Hume refused a business offer that would have made him a wealthy man. Each did what he did in reverence to the call of a destiny he each felt he had to fulfill. Each pursued his destiny with dramatically clear decisions that affected the entire texture of his life.

We cannot help but admire men and women who have been willing to listen to a call from within and respond to it deeply. Each of these men felt that there was something he had to do with his life. There was a unique destiny they had to fulfill and they did it. If they had not responded, they would not have been true to themselves.

Is there a unique destiny that calls to each of us?

> *Every act and every inquiry,*
> *and similarly, every action and pursuit*
> *is thought to aim at some good,*
> *and for this reason the good has rightly been declared to be*
> *that at which all things aim.*
> *A flute player, a sculptor or an artist has a function or activity....*
> *So it seems to be for man....*
> *Have the carpenter and the tanner*
> *certain functions or activities and man none?*
> *Is he born without a function?*
> —Aristotle, *Nichomachean Ethics*

What Is Our End?

Aristotle's theory of ethics centered around his belief that human beings, like everything in nature, had an end or culminating point toward which life is persistently drawn. The hand, he said, obviously has a function, as does a foot or an eye. Aristotle asks if it is possible that we, as a people, are made up of parts with various functions and yet we, as a whole, have no function, no purpose for being.

Psychologist Dr. Victor Frankl, who survived the experience of Auschwitz, said that the people who best handled the trauma of the death camps were those who somehow saw that even in the horror there was some sort of meaning, some ultimate spiritual purpose or end. Jesus is crucified on the cross. It looks like a tragedy, yet there is a purpose in the event. As we each face our individual problems we need to see that there is a purpose for whatever we are experiencing, whether we see it or not.

Many artists, entrepreneurs, entertainers, and contented and suc-
cessful people know from an early age that there is a function or
purpose that the whole of their lives is about.

The more clearly we can pursue the function we understand to
be uniquely our function, the more our lives seem to have meaning
and purpose. Those who impeccably pursue their destinies are often
the happiest people, though they might choose to remain single, turn
down wealth, or even be crucified.

The *Course* talks about our accepting our function in the following way:

> *"Once you accept His plan*
> *as the one function that you would fulfill,*
> *there will be nothing else*
> *the Holy Spirit will not arrange*
> *for you without effort.*
> *He will go before you making straight your path,*
> *and leaving in your way no stones to trip on,*
> *and no obstacles to bar your way.*
> *Nothing you need will be denied you.*
> *Not one seeming difficulty*
> *but will melt away before you reach it.*
> *You need take thought for nothing,*
> *careless of everything except*
> *the only purpose that you would fulfill.*
> *As that was given you,*
> *so will its fulfillment be."*
> —T.404; T-20.IV.8:4-9

Jesus had great power. Had he wanted to, he could have become
another Alexander or Genghis Khan, yet from the age of twelve, if
not before, he was clear about a higher calling. His mission was greater
than that of earthly kings. His destiny was true wealth. He chose
to do something really marvelous. He recognized his own identity.
He recognized Heaven as his home and God as his Father. Clear
about the Kingdom of Heaven itself, he pursued his destiny with an
impeccable clarity that left its mark on all of humankind.

It Is Finished

"Great is the art of beginning
but greater is the art of ending."
—Henry Wadsworth Longfellow

What great words are the final words of Jesus on the cross: *"It is finished."* How many of us upon reaching the end of our lives will be able to say, "It is finished." There are many interesting last words of many great men and women, but those are the greatest of all the last words.

Jesus had done what he came to do. He did it in only three short years. How many of us upon the completion of ten or twenty times that many years will be able to get to the end and say: "It is finished." It is done. I did what I came here to do.

At the time of my death, I should like to be able to say, "It is finished." Wouldn't you? Do you not want to feel that you have done what you came here to do?

There are some people who might argue that Jesus on the cross had not completed his task. Christianity would go through many years of persecution. And what he had to teach would be grossly misinterpreted. There are millions who still need to see what he saw. Other men and women would have to take over. Yet, clearly, in that time and space he had done what he had come to do. So he could say: *"It is finished."*

Think about how good you feel when a task you have undertaken has been seen through to the end. The paper is completed, the craft is made, the degree is attained, the house is built, the book is finished. We all need the feeling of accomplishment. We need to undertake projects and complete them.

Discovering Our Destiny

Those who are most in touch with destiny feel it is not of their own making. It is something that has been given to them. To discover one's destiny is not to make up something; it is to find something.

"The meaning of existence is not invented but rather detected."
—Victor Frankl

Our purpose does not have to be something grand. We do not have to become a world leader or a hero. Our purpose may be to be a good mother or father, an effective teacher, a wise administrator, or a master builder. It may be to contribute to community growth and betterment, or we may be called to fulfill life through some form of artistic expression like music, writing, drawing, or painting.

Whatever is asked of us, when we fulfill our destiny and do what we are supposed to do, we are fulfilling God's will as well. Destiny has meaning when it is God's will as well as ours. Each of us is called to help in building a harmonious universe. We are all called to forgive and to help find the entrance to the Kingdom of Heaven.

If what you are doing is not fulfilling, there is no need to be upset. As we respond even more deeply than we already have to our life, we automatically begin to fulfill our mission more clearly.

"He who has a 'why' can forbear any 'how.'"
—Friedrich Nietzsche

Those who pay attention to the call of destiny, those who stop long enough to get quiet enough to listen to the voice of God, hear a clear and distinct call. With a sense of purpose, mission, and destiny the accomplishment of any task is easy.

The treasure hidden in the field, the pearl of great price is nothing less than our work; the alchemy of our lives is what it is all about. Seeing helps us to achieve and enables us to help others.

First Be Rich toward God

We may pray to God for money if we are hungry or have a great need, but it is more important that the spirit of abundance fill our hearts. Pray for inspiration and get out of the way. Pray that the wealth of Heaven might fill you. Do not worry about how you are going to live. Work on doing what you are supposed to be doing. Go ahead. Get started. Do it. Move forward. Get something done on the project you understand you are supposed to be working on. Do not let the issue of personal survival overwhelm you.

There is no reason why the ideal may not be attained. It is possible to have happy relationships. If you want a happy marriage why not have one? Why should you settle for anything less? It is possible to do what you want to do and get paid for it. Why should you not do it? It is possible to find the entrance to the Kingdom of Heaven. Why should you not find it?

There comes a time in each of the hero stories when the hero must awaken from the darkness of his own ego. In doing so, new mysteries are revealed, not only those concerning his own destiny, but often of humanity at large, as when Aeneas learned of the destiny of Rome.

Succeeding in our task, we can help others succeed at theirs. Once the hero has fulfilled the task he was supposed to fulfill, even greater meaning and purpose opens up before him. At the end of the journey there is often a marriage, the symbol of completion. The princess is the paragon of beauty, the answer to all desire, the bliss-bestowing goal of the quest, the incarnation of perfection. Christian of *Pilgrim's Progress* finds at last the entrance to the Celestial City. The Kingdom of Heaven and the entrance to it are available to us. The moment we respond to the call we are there.

As he accepts his destiny, the hero becomes a teacher of God. It is inevitable. The whole world of natural experience, the heavens and hells of traditional religious beliefs, the systems of glossing, and the whole of the habitual and traditional world fall away and we can see a state beyond the vicissitudes of time — a space of ultimate wealth, abundance, and uninterrupted paradise.

> *"The end is something that proves everything."*
> —Anonymous

Our task is deeper than any soap opera, ego game, or wandering in the personal unconscious.

> *"... the end of hell is guaranteed.*
> *Begin in hopefulness,*
> *for we have reached the turning point*
> *at which the road becomes far easier.*
> *And now the way is short that yet we travel.*
> *We are close indeed to the appointed ending of the dream."*
> —W.214; W-pI.122.8:1-4

Postscript

What's Missing?

Much more could be said about the importance of the Holy Spirit, so much more I think it worthwhile to devote an entire book to the topic.

What Else?

If you have enjoyed this book you might enjoy a subscription to:

On Course:
Bi-weekly Inspiration
for the Inner Journey

On Course is published twenty-six times a year and costs $2.00 per issue for second-class mail or $2.75 a week for delivery by first-class mail inside a protective envelope.

A subscription to *On Course* can be ordered through:

Interfaith Fellowship
459 Carol Drive
Monroe, NY 10950-9565
Tel.: 800-275-4809

In addition to the magazine we also publish yearly *A Course in Miracles Directory, Resource Guide and Scrapbook*

Copies of *A Course in Miracles* can be ordered through Interfaith Fellowship for $25 plus $2.00 for shipping.

Many larger bookstores and New Age bookstores carry the *Course.* You may also obtain the *Course* through:

> The Foundation for Inner Peace
> P.O. Box 1104
> Glen Ellen, CA 95442-1104

Additional Reading

Coit, Lee. *Listening*. Available from Las Brisas Retreat Center, PO Box 500 Wildomar, CA 92595-0500. Lee is also the author of *Listening Still*.

Ferrini, Paul. *The Twelve Steps of Forgiveness*. Heartways Press (PO Box 418, Santa Fe, NM 87504-0418), 1991. Paul is also the author of *The Wisdom of the Self: Authentic Experience and the Journey to Wholeness* and other books.

Hotchkiss, Burt. *Your Owners Manual*. Fernwood Management, 25441 Rice Rd., Sweet Home, OR 97386-9620.

Jampolsky, Jerry, M.D. *Love Is Letting Go of Fear*. New York: Bantam, 1984. Attitudinal Healing, 19 Main St., Belvedere–Tiburon CA 94920-2507.

————. *Teach Only Love: The Seven Principles of Attitudinal Healing*. New York: Bantam, 1984.

Perry, Robert. *Introduction to "A Course in Miracles."* Available from Robert Perry, PO Box 4238, West Sedona, AZ 86340-4238. Robert is also the author of *The Elder Brother: Jesus in "A Course in Miracles"* and an ongoing series of booklets on the *Course*.

Raub, John Jacob. *Who Told You That You Were Naked? Freedom from Judgment, Guilt, and Fear of Punishment*. New York: Crossroad, 1992.

Singh, Tara. *A Course in Miracles: A Gift for All Mankind*. Los Angeles: Life Action Press, 1992. Tara Singh is also the author of many other books. Foundation for Life Action, 902 S. Burnside Ave., Los Angeles, CA 90036.

Wapnick, Kenneth. *A Talk Given on "A Course in Miracles."* 1990. A good introduction to the *Course*. 119 pp. Available from Foundation for "A Course in Miracles," RR 2, Box 71, Roscoe, NY 12776-9506.

————. *Absence from Felicity: The Story of Helen Schucman and Her Scribing of "A Course in Miracles."* Roscoe, N.Y.: Foundation for "A Course in Miracles," 1991. 521 pp.

————. *Forgiveness and Jesus: The Meeting Place of "A Course in Miracles and Christianity."* Roscoe, N.Y.: Foundation for "A Course in Miracles," 1983. Addresses the misunderstanding of traditional Christianity, separating these from the teachings of the *Course*. 348 pp.

Williamson, Marianne. *A Return to Love: Reflections on the Principles of "A Course in Miracles."* New York: HarperCollins, 1992. Thirty-seven weeks on the best-seller list. Miracles Projects, 1550 N. Hayworth, Ave., Los Angeles, CA 90046-3337.